The Confederate Dirty War

The Confederate Dirty War

Arson, Bombings, Assassination and Plots for Chemical and Germ Attacks on the Union

JANE SINGER

McFarland & Company, Inc., Publishers
Jefferson, North Carolina, and London

LIBRARY OF CONGRESS CATALOGUING-IN-PUBLICATION DATA

Singer, Jane.
   The Confederate dirty war : arson, bombings, assassination and
plots for chemical and germ attacks on the Union / Jane Singer.
      p.   cm.
   Includes bibliographical references and index.

   ISBN 0-7864-1973-3 (softcover : 50# alkaline paper) ∞

   1. Confederate States of America — Politics and government.
2. United States — History — Civil War, 1861–1865 — Underground
movements.   3. Political violence — Confederate States of
America — History.   4. Political violence — United States —
History — 19th century.   5. Subversive activities — Confederate
States of America — History.   6. Subversive activities — United
States — History — 19th century.   7. Arson — Political aspects —
United States — History — 19th century.   8. Bombings — United
States — History — 19th century.   9. Assassination — United
States — History — 19th century.   10. Weapons of mass
destruction — United States — History — 19th century.   I. Title.
E487.S55   2005
973.7'3013 — dc22   2005009222

British Library cataloguing data are available

Cover photograph © 2005 PhotoSpin

Manufactured in the United States of America

McFarland & Company, Inc., Publishers
   Box 611, Jefferson, North Carolina 28640
      www.mcfarlandpub.com

To Morton Aaron Singer and Frances Brown Singer:
In memoriam and eternal love

Acknowledgments

If there has been a single, guiding force throughout my descent into the dark and fanatical world of a most "uncivil" war, it is the esteemed Lincoln assassination scholar Dr. James O. Hall. It is to this "paterfamilias" of Lincoln assassination research that a debt is forever owed. His wisdom, guidance, inspiration and friendship are valued beyond measure.

For their love and support, I thank my husband Charles Eckstein, my beloved daughter Jessica Eve Masser, my brother James Singer, Lisa Singer, Miles and Raleigh Singer, Missy Eckstein, Ken and Cynthia Eckstein, Hariet and Stanley Eckstein, Judy Oppenheimer, Jerry Oppenheimer, Larry Masser, Susan Grant, Dan Halperin, Mike Nelson, Susan Chieco, Elizabeth Feiss, Judy Messinger, Captain Joseph Asher, and Susanne and Marty Malles. I also thank Tina and Angus who have happily shared my long, irregular hours.

To able scholars Edward Steers, Jr., David Winfred Gaddy, Robert Scott Davis, Jr., Betty J. Ownsbey, Laurie Verge, Nancy Disher Baird, Deborah and Geo Rule, and Joan L. Chaconas; my special appreciation.

And to Charles Higham, a fellow traveler into the endless rabbit holes of history, I am ever grateful.

Special and heartfelt thanks to Beverly Carrigan who entrusted me with the task and privilege of illuminating the life and death of Felix Stidger.

And to Nancy Clayton, I am grateful for the opportunity to share the last sad days of Felix Stidger with readers.

Thanks also to Joann Stidger Becker, Richard Willing, Bill O'Brian, Lynda Robinson, Woody West, Andrew Herrmann, Michael Musick, Wayne T. DeCesar, Linda McCurdy, Lynda Crist, John and Ruth Ann Coski, Cara Griggs, Susan Deupree Jones, Sarina Bean, William Pugsley, Heather W. Milne, Vaughn Stanley, Jeffery Smart, Lavonne Markham, Mark Frazel, Carey Lundin, Engel Brothers Media, William Hanchett, Tom Shroder, Linda Harney McDonald, Ellen Jane Hollis, Richard Nathan Leigh and Liza Gerberding for their help.

The family of Professor Richard Sears McCulloch has been more than generous. To Richard McCulloch, Anna McCulloch, Duncan McCulloch, Professor Charles Hardy, and all other family members, I hope I have presented a true and balanced portrait of your esteemed relation.

Table of Contents

"The authorities of the Confederate States appear, by the record, to have exhausted all possible efforts for humane and honorable warfare...."

Lieutenant John William Headley, CSA, second in command of the plot to destroy New York City.

Preface

Just steps from the northeast perimeter of Ground Zero is the site of the old Astor House Hotel on lower Broadway in New York City. There, on November 25, 1864, a band of Confederate agents launched an arson attack in an effort to reduce hotels, homes and civilians to ashes.

Scattered throughout the historical record is incontrovertible evidence of the Confederate plot to burn New York and other projects aimed at noncombatants in the Civil War. Among them were:

- A bio-terror attempt to spread yellow fever and smallpox
- Plans to poison New York City's water supply
- An effort to overthrow the federal government by the treasonous secret order known as the Sons of Liberty by means of arson and assassination
- The attempted takeover and destruction of St. Albans, Vermont, by Confederate agents
- The perfection of a chemical weapon meant to suffocate and incinerate northern civilians
- A planned decapitation of the Federal government by assassination and the demolition of the White House

Some of the projects failed, but the intent of the plotters was always clear: kill, terrify and demoralize.

The Confederate defeat at Gettysburg in the summer of 1863, followed swiftly by the fall of Vicksburg, changed the course of the Civil War. When in March of 1864 Lieutenant General Ulysses S. Grant was appointed commander of all Union armies, General Robert E. Lee's forces were doomed. "Cornered and in extremis," rogue scientists, biologists, explosives experts and saboteurs proposed and promised projects guaranteed to "bring terror and consternation" to masses of innocent civilians in the North "solely to create death." Remarkably, many Union civilians knew they too had been targeted by a dying Confederacy as it spiraled toward destruction.

While aspects of terror plots in the Civil War have been written about in fine, scholarly works such as *Come Retribution* by General William A. Tidwell, James O. Hall and David Winfred Gaddy, *April '65* by General Tidwell, *Blood on the Moon* by Edward Steers, Jr., and *The Man Who Tried to Burn New York* by Nat Brandt, the vast body of mainstream scholarship has all but omitted the study of a hidden Civil War.

The search for extant evidence and documentation has been a long journey, for much has been destroyed or buried in the half-light of obfuscation, omission and denial.

I have relied on the indispensable 128 volume record of the U.S. War Department, *The War of the Rebellion: A Compilation of the Official Records of the Union and the Confederate Armies*, as well as the Confederate Compiled Service Records, telegrams collected by the Secretary of War, and the Union Provost Marshal's Civilian Files housed in the National Archives in Washington, D.C.

Primary source material found in newspapers and firsthand accounts rather than twenty-first century interpretations of facts and missions have been vital to my research.

I have benefited greatly from several important collections of private papers and documents housed in the Museum of the Confederacy in Richmond, Virginia; the Bermuda National Library; the Library of Virginia; the Virginia Historical Society; the Columbia University Archives; the Chicago Historical Society; the Kentucky Historical Society; the Leyburn Library of Washington and Lee University; the University of Kentucky Special Collections Archives; the Missouri Historical Society; and the Surratt House Museum and James O. Hall Research Center in Clinton, Maryland. I have also used unpublished materials from the families of Professor Richard Sears McCulloch,* William Stephen Deupree, and Detective Felix Grundy Stidger.

"History," warned Abraham Lincoln, "is not history unless it is the truth." What follows is history.

---

*Richard Sears McCulloh and his brother John McCulloh went back to the ancestral spelling of the family name, McCulloch, following the war, probably around 1878, with the hope that future generations would follow. They have.

ONE

The War in Context

"A strange, sad war."[1]

As dusk descended on Richmond, Virginia, and wary soldiers patrolled the scorched, rubble-strewn streets, an enemy combatant approached the headquarters of the occupying forces with an urgent warning. An attack was planned on the most prominent and beloved symbol of the United States: The White House. The attack was timed to occur when the President and his cabinet were sure to be inside. And worse, an explosives expert had already been dispatched on the mission. But even as officials failed to deter the president's return to Washington from his victory trip to Richmond, by an act of providence or simple accident, the bomber was captured just 14 miles from his intended target.

Two days later, in the nation's capital, the White House stood unscathed, resplendent, its wood, brick and polished stone intact. Amid sounds of trumpet serenades and grateful prayers, weary residents heard their president announce the long, punishing ordeal was finally over. It was April 1865, the last month of the Civil War.

It was hardly a "civil" war. By the end, 620,000 husbands, fathers, sons, and a president lay dead. Initial excitement and the hope that the war would be quick with "the striding wind of nations with new rain, new lightning" were only part of the story.[2]

The internecine conflict invaded backyards, farms and cities. Days and weeks became months and, then, impossibly, years. And as the war crawled toward a final bloody spring, disease, desperation and growing battlefield defeats fed fanatical sensibilities.

Not unexpected, these desperate measures. Until 1863, no code of conduct, no laws of war, existed. The sons and grandsons of "sunshine

3

patriots" had never before fought each other. And well before the Civil War, a gaping moral divide separated the nation. Many in the North had never seen a plantation or owned another human being. Fewer still in the primarily rural South had ventured above the Mason-Dixon line and strongly believed in the supreme right of their individual states to govern them. And, as the founders had proclaimed, the profitable institution of slavery was necessary.

Mythologies and glorifications abound: "The South, they said," wrote southern historian Robert Selph Henry, "burdened with the defense of the anachronism of slavery ... rebelled." And what a tangle it was, as Senators and Congressmen, friends, classmates, neighbors and political rivals became sworn enemies.[3]

Ordinary boys, "Johnny Reb" and "Billy Yank," some barely out of their teens, followed orders and killed an enemy who looked remarkably like themselves. If they survived disease, imprisonment and the battlefield, they came home. For some, home was a few feet away, for others, hundreds of miles. And when it began, many dreamed it over quickly. "Has it come so soon to this?" mused then United States commander Robert E. Lee.[4]

On February 9, 1861, President Franklin Pierce's former Secretary of War, the elegant, patrician Senator Jefferson Davis of Mississippi, was elected President of the newly formed Confederacy, termed "a government having nothing with everything to provide" by Robert Selph Henry.[5] But in a few short months, the nation with nothing had become a formidable foe.

By March of 1861, seven slave-holding states, outraged by Lincoln's threat to abolish slavery, had seceded from the Union. During the following month, the war officially began when General Pierre Gustave Toutant Beauregard from the newly formed Confederacy opened fire with 50 cannons on Fort Sumter in Charleston, South Carolina.

A defiant Virginia immediately seceded. Neighboring pro-secessionist Maryland attempted to follow. Fearing the nation's capitol would fall to the Confederates if Maryland joined the Confederacy, President Lincoln suspended the writ of habeas corpus which forbid arbitrary and unlawful imprisonments and jailed Maryland legislators before they could vote for secession. To further inflame many Marylanders, Lincoln imposed martial law throughout the state, engendering bitter hatreds that would last for generations. "My Maryland," the poem that became the state song written by native son Charles Ryder Randall in 1861, speaks volumes:

> The despot's heel is on thy shore, Maryland!
> Thou wilt not crook to his control...
> Better the shot, the blade, the bowl, than crucifixion of the Soul
> She is not dead, nor deaf, nor dumb–Huzza!
> She spurns the Northern scum...
> Maryland! My Maryland!

Five weeks later, Arkansas, Tennessee and North Carolina spurned the "despot" to join South Carolina, Mississippi, Florida, Alabama, Georgia, Louisiana and Texas. The brittle union of states had crumbled.

Abraham Lincoln vowed to continue the Civil War until slavery was abolished in spite of his faith in "the better angels of our nature."[6] With each passionate declaration of intent, each presumed statement of autocratic defiance, outraged Confederates protested the actions of "King" Lincoln.[7]

Undeterred, President Lincoln continued to enact measures he believed would end the war. His enemies viewed the measures to come as unendurable punishments. They arrived with a vengeance.

On September 24, 1862, Lincoln issued a proclamation suspending the writ of habeas corpus:

> All Rebels and insurgents, their aiders and abettors within the United States, and all persons discouraging volunteer enlistments, resisting military drafts, or guilty of any disloyal practice ... shall be subject to martial law and liable to trial and punishment by Courts Martial or Military Commission.... In respect to all persons arrested, or who are now, or hereafter during the rebellion shall be, imprisoned in any fort, camp, arsenal, military prison, or other place of confinement by any military authority of by the sentence of any Court Martial or Military commission.[8]

On September 15, 1863, Lincoln suspended the writ throughout the Union.[9]

Finally, buoyed by the Union victory at Antietam, Lincoln reluctantly issued the final Emancipation Proclamation on January 1, 1863, forever changing the socio-economic construct of the South (the first had been issued on September 22, 1862). And just as the blistering Confederate defeat at Gettysburg in July of 1863 is usually cited as a turning point in the Civil War, the issuance of the Emancipation Proclamation, the fears it engendered, and its ultimate obliteration of the South's labor force, was indeed a Rubicon, an eventual demise of a profitable economic system, the very fabric of plantation existence.

"A restoration of the Union has now been rendered forever impossible," Jefferson Davis told the Confederate Congress eleven days after the proclamation became official. He went on to say that it was a "measure by which several millions of human beings of an inferior race, peaceful and contented laborers in their sphere, are doomed to extermination, while at the same time they are encouraged to a general assassination of their masters."[10]

Calling the Proclamation "the most execrable measure in the history of guilty man," President Jefferson Davis and his followers were further enraged to learn that it called for the enlistment of black soldiers into the military. As a result, atrocities by some Confederate troops abounded. If captured, a black soldier faced torture, execution, or in the eyes of some, a fate worse than death—a return to slavery.[11]

Deeply disturbed by these atrocities, Lincoln issued an "Order of Retaliation." It stated, "The government of the United States will give the same protection to all its soldiers, and if the enemy shall sell or enslave anyone because of his color, the offense shall be punished by retaliation upon the enemy's prisoners in our possession. It is therefore ordered that for every [Black] soldier of the United States killed in violation of the laws of war, a rebel soldier shall be executed; and for everyone enslaved by the enemy or sold into slavery, a rebel soldier shall be placed at hard labor...."[12]

In response to these perceived outrages, Fifth Column societies, an "enemy within," took hold in the North. Further fanning the flames; fueling hatred of the anti-slavery policies of President Lincoln, and urging resistance to conscription, southern Northerners known as Copperheads, or "doughfaces," vehemently opposed the conflict at all costs. The press, abetted by sympathetic Northern newspapers and coded messages in unsuspecting pro-administration publications, also played a role in fomenting dissent and worse.

Growing war weariness in the North and the smell of defeat in the South finally split the Democratic Party cleanly into two camps. The "war" Democrats supported Lincoln and the war effort, while the "peace" Democrats (Copperheads) favored a negotiated settlement—retaining slavery and the Confederacy's right to exist. While not all peace Democrats were sympathetic to the secret plots of seditious organizations known successively as the Knights of the Golden Circle, the Order of American Knights, and the Sons of Liberty, an unsettling number joined a hidden enemy.

Their progenitors fomented plans to create a Northwest Confederacy. Cells or "castles" were activated in Ohio, Indiana, Illinois, Missouri and Kentucky. Replete with elaborate rituals, pledges, secret signs and coded symbols, many in this brotherhood of professionals, politicians, judges and scientists were committed to the destruction of the United States and the expansion of slavery. To this end, efforts were made to arm insurgents, release Confederate prisoners and create mayhem in the North.

Fed by the anger and helplessness felt by thousands as men were ordered to the front lines, in some Union cities "Treason ... everywhere, reigned, ... bold, defiant and active with impunity;" Illinois Democrat John A. McClernand warned in a letter to Abraham Lincoln.[13]

In March of 1863, Lincoln passed the First Conscription Act, making all men between the ages of 20 and 45 eligible for duty. Families who were able paid a fee of $300 to hire a substitute to fight for their loved ones. But many could not earn the money if they worked solidly for two years, so thousands of able-bodied young men trudged off to war. Resistance to conscription was inevitable, as were riots.

A worried Lincoln looked north to New York, a city that *was* surprisingly "bold, defiant and active with impunity."

Governed by Copperheads, fire-eaters all, New York teemed with unemployed immigrants living in abject squalor. The city was ripe for riot. It was on this stew of unrest of inflammatory rhetoric and racism that anti-administration sentiment fed and finally boiled.

On July 13, 1863, angry immigrant New Yorkers, resentful of forced conscription and enraged by the newly freed slaves who swarmed east and threatened their menial jobs, went on a rampage of lynching and destruction incited by those who warned that cities "would be overrun with Negroes, they will compete with you and bring down your wages, you will have to work with them, eat with them, your wives and children must associate with theirs and you and your families will be degraded to their level."[14]

The bloody riots, the leaders of New York claimed, were President Lincoln's fault. On July 14, amid the burning, looting and killing in the city, Edward S. Sanford of the U.S. Military Telegraph Service wrote to Secretary of War Stanton, begging for help:

Sir: You may judge of the capacity at headquarters here when every effort cannot extract any more information than I have forwarded. Excuse me for saying that this mob is testing the government nearly as strongly as the Southern rebellion. If you cannot enforce the draft here, it will not be enforced elsewhere. The example will prove contagious, and similar events transpire in every large city. If you send sufficient forces here to demonstrate the power of the government, its effect will reach every part of the country, and one settlement answer for the whole. Immediate action is necessary, or the government and country will be disgraced.[15]

By contrast, John B. Jones, a Confederate war clerk in Richmond, was jubilant:

We have awful good news from New York: an INSURRECTION, the loss of many lives, extensive pillage and burning, with a suspension of the conscription! ... If the insurrection in New York lives, and resistance to conscription should be general in the North, our people will take fresh hope, and make renewed efforts to beat back the mighty armies of the foe-suffering and more than decimated, as we are.[16]

The jubilation was short-lived.

An increasingly desperate Confederacy, outnumbered and out-gunned with desertions growing by the hundreds, faced a stark reality. The Union was still intact, swollen with new recruits and winning the fight. As Jefferson Davis and his brilliant, indispensable Secretary of State Judah P. Benjamin lobbied their Congress to provide more funds for clandestine operations, an aborted Union raid on Richmond hardened the Confederacy's resolve to win the war by any means necessary.

On February 28, 1864, just outside Richmond, Ulric Dahlgren, a young, one-legged Union colonel, was shot in the back by Confederate soldiers and killed instantly. This tragic but not uncommon event caused a massive concussion throughout the south. Dahlgren's death aborted a mission that might well have ended the war.

Driven to take cover in a blinding rain, Dahlgren and his men were separated from their superior, Brigadier General H. Judson Kilpatrick. The objective of the Dahlgren-Kilpatrick raid was two-pronged: the liberation of Union soldiers trapped in the infamous Belle Isle Prison Camp and the subsequent destruction of Richmond. Both failed.

A paper found on Dahlgren's body by a thirteen-year-old boy revealed that Dahlgren carried orders to burn and destroy the Confederate capitol.

The order further stated, "Do not allow the Rebel leader Davis and his traitorous crew to escape."[17]

A second document was even more specific. "The men [the liberated prisoners and soldiers] must keep together and well in hand. And once in the city it must be destroyed and Jeff Davis and the cabinet killed."[18]

The papers quickly reached the desk of Confederate secretary of war James A. Seddon and finally President Jefferson Davis. Although they were unsigned, the documents appeared to have been authorized at the highest levels of the Union government.

"The blood boils with indignation in the veins of every officer and man," Robert E. Lee wrote, "as they read the account of [Dahlgren's] barbarous and inhuman plot...."[19]

Southern papers howled. "What would have been the condition of Richmond this day week one week ago had Dahlgren succeeded? Imagine ten to twelve brutal soldiers released from captivity ... picture the smoking ruins, the dishonored women and the murdered men of Richmond."[20]

Called a forgery or worse, a confabulation by an irate Northern public, twenty-first century historian Dr. James O. Hall labored to authenticate the papers. Hall proved conclusively that a misspelling of Dahlgren's name was not a Confederate forgery, but the fault of bleeding ink and folded paper. To Southerners, the authenticity of the Dahlgren papers was never in question.

Whether or not the orders came directly from President Lincoln, as some historians have concluded, the Davis government abandoned any reservations they might otherwise have had about waging a war of terror against the North. President Lincoln, once viewed as a possible hostage, a pawn in a desperate effort to force the Union to capitulate, was now a moving target.

Retribution remained a challenge. With Northern armies sweeping across embattled Virginia and General Sherman's troops amassing in the hardscrabble mountains of north Georgia preparing to march to the sea, Confederate leaders ordered their agents across the Canadian border far to the north. "Any clandestine operator attempting to work against the United States," wrote authors James O. Hall, David Winfred Gaddy and William Tidwell, "would be bound to recognize the opportunities provided by this combination of friendly people, a tolerant government and advantageous geography."[21]

Also of importance was the need for the Davis government to "keep abreast of the status of British and provincial policy towards the Confederates...."[22]

Officially neutral, Canada was governed by representatives of the British nation and, like England, decidedly pro–Confederate in the Civil War. Toronto was full of Southern refugees. Montreal, London, St. Catherine's and Windsor were havens for spies, "destructionists" (explosive experts) and arsonists.

While President Jefferson Davis had established a Confederate presence in Canada as early as 1861 for the purpose of moving people and dispatches, formulating "peace" plans and establishing a diplomatic post by early 1864, and with a history of Yankee-hating sentiments stretching back eighty years (many English-speaking Canadian denizens' families had fought the British and French in America), the porous and unguarded Canadian border posed a danger to the Union.

Impotent peace plans, one sided and self-serving at best, were floated by the Davis government. The South would never give up its slave-holding economy and way of life, and Lincoln would never accept anything but full reunification without slavery. With cries for revenge growing louder, Jefferson Davis turned to his secretary of state for a solution.

Born in the West Indies, Judah P. Benjamin grew up in South Carolina and practiced law in New Orleans. In 1852, he was elected to the Senate from Louisiana. Called "a seal-sleek, black-eyed lawyer and epicure," with a "quick, shrewd, fluid mind,"[23] Benjamin served as Jefferson Davis' secretary of war and secretary of state. Much has been written about the enigmatic, witty, Benjamin, a villain to some, a hero and helpmate to others including Jefferson Davis and his family. Myth and reality, often seen through an anti–Semitic scrim, obscure Benjamin's role in the last years of the war. And the riddle of Davis' dependence on the judgment and clandestine maneuverings of Benjamin is still being debated.[24]

One of the few biographies of Benjamin offers sometimes definitive takes on the nature of the relationship.

"Benjamin served Davis as his Sephardic ancestors had served the kings of Europe for hundreds of years," wrote Eli Evans. "An insecure President Davis was able to trust him completely, because among other things, no Jew could ever challenge him for leadership of the Confederacy," Evans suggests. Perhaps it was Benjamin's sheer brilliance and loyalty that bound the men, most likely the latter. In the last year of the war, when Benjamin acted with autonomy, often making decisions on his own, the Confederate president was forever grateful.[25]

With Davis' full approval and invaluable signature, Judah P. Benjamin allotted $1 million in secret service monies from the Confederate treasury to fund the last "projects" of the war. "Request No. 32, dated April 25, 1864, was for one million dollars [in gold] for "Secret Service.""[26]

In order to establish a network of secret agents in Canada to join forces with Northerners sympathetic to the Southern cause, President Jefferson Davis appointed fellow Mississippian Jacob Thompson to head the operation. The Official Records (OR) contain a directive from President

Jacob Thompson, leader of the Confederate commissioners in Canada (Library of Congress).

Jefferson Davis to Thompson, former Secretary of the Interior under President James Buchanan and a die-hard secessionist rumored to have warned the people of Charleston a ship was arriving to re-supply Fort Sumter.

Encyclopedia of the United States editor Marc Grossman speculated that Thompson "indirectly influenced the blocking of the ship and firing on Fort Sumter on April 12, 1861, that ignited the American Civil War." When Thompson resigned his cabinet post, Jefferson Davis summoned him to Canada: "Hon. Jacob Thompson: If your engagements will permit you to accept service abroad [Canada] for the next six months, please come here [Richmond] immediately. Jefferson Davis"

"I hereby direct you to proceed at once to Canada," Davis wrote Thompson on April 27, 1864, soon after the failed raid. "There to carry out such instructions as you have received from me verbally, in such manner as shall seem most likely to the furtherance of the interest of the Confederate States of America which have been entrusted to you."[27]

Soon, Thompson joined Richmond newspaper editor Nathaniel Beverly Tucker, European "assassination bureau" proponent George Sanders, military agent Thomas Hines, former Alabama senator Clement Claiborne Clay, and University of Virginia law professor James P. Holcombe.

His purses bulging with gold, Thompson recruited like-minded Northerners to perform acts of sabotage. In spite of the fact that uneasy Union loyalists caught wind of these lethal cabals and sent word to local military posts for men brave enough to infiltrate the cells, the plots went forward.

Soldiers attached to the infamous Confederate raider John Hunt Morgan, disgruntled politicos and chemists, Sons of Liberty, leaders of the Northwest Confederacy, arsonists, and a zealous Kentucky physician assembled in Canada. Added to the mix were informants, double agents and escaped prisoners. In fine hotels, over good cigars and better brandy, they plotted the destruction of the Federal government.

Out of Canada came Dr. Luke Pryor Blackburn's plot to spread yellow fever throughout the North; the raid by a group of Confederate agents on the village of St. Albans, Vermont; Robert C. Martin and John William Headley's plan to reduce New York City to ashes; the Sons of Liberty's proposed uprisings as well as the poisoning

Clement Claiborne Clay, Confederate commissioner in Canada (Library of Congress).

of New York City's water supply and the bombing of the Croton Dam. And, according to some modern Civil War historians, the assassination of Abraham Lincoln.

There were warnings. Union authorities were getting wind of trouble, but only in the form of vague and unspecified threats.

By November 26, 1864, Colonel B.J. Sweet was commanding the headquarters of Camp Douglas in Chicago. He wrote an urgent dispatch to General H.W. Wessells, Inspector and Commissary General of Prisoners in Washington, D.C.: "Mr. Thompson still remains in Canada plotting against the peace and safety of our Northern cities and communities and planning injurious enterprises against us of a character, and conducted in a manner unknown to the laws of war. The proof against him is positive and accessible...."[28]

The warnings were ignored. When Confederate agent Reverend Kensey Johns Stewart vehemently opposed a bio-terror attack he believed would surely invoke the wrath of God, President Davis did nothing to prevent it from going forward.

Robert E. Lee objected to yet another secret project endorsed by Confederate leadership in Canada and Richmond, not on its morality, but on the grounds that the men involved were not right for the job. If the qualifications of the agents worried Lee, there were no such concerns across the border. Instead, there was anger.

Jacob Thompson vented his spleen to Secretary Judah P. Benjamin over the failed plot to burn New York. After a careful review of aborted projects and failed insurrections, Jacob Thompson was ordered out of the field.

Undeterred, Benjamin and Davis sent Brigadier General Edwin Gray Lee to replace Thompson in Canada. Soon, a more lethal chemical incendiary was readied in Richmond, the plot to bomb the White House went forward, and actor and Confederate agent John Wilkes Booth prepared his action team, in case all else failed.

Were these men fanatics seeking revenge for bygone atrocities and the destruction of their slave-holding economy? The answers are as varied and complex as the men themselves. One thing is certain: They were not common soldiers merely following orders. Some were actively seeking revenge. Others leapt at the chance to mastermind the plots, remaining in the shadows and directing foot soldiers to do their bidding. Some were privateers looking for a boon from a Confederacy that was slowly bleeding to death. Some were disgruntled scientists using the war to enhance their own extremity. Others were merely foot soldiers obeying commands. Almost none had lost loved ones in the war. All were unrepentant.

"It is a matter of no importance whether the acts proposed to be done ... accord with the usages and principles of modern civilized warfare," Williamson Simpson Oldham, a senator in the Confederate Congress, wrote in an unpublished memoir written after the war.[29] In 1865, he promised Jefferson Davis, "We can devastate the country of the enemy and fill its people with terror and consternation."[30]

Even the most vilified of Northern generals, William Tecumseh Sherman, emboldened by his commander-in-chief to lay waste to the South, agonized over his actions: "Think of how cruel men have become in war, when even your papa has to do such acts," he wrote to his daughter Minnie on the bloody Christmas of 1864 as his troops marched through Georgia. "Pray every night that the war may end. Hundreds of children like yourself are daily taught to curse my name, and every night thousands kneel in prayer and beseech the almighty to consign me to perdition."[31]

But for some Confederates "consigned to perdition," risking the curses of children, there were no rules and no such agonies.

TWO

In the Absence of Rules

"When is war not a war? When it was carried on by methods of barbarism...."

Sir Henry Campbell-Bannerman*

"To surprise a peaceful town and shoot down people in the streets ... is not civilized war, it is that of savages."

The Colonial Standard, October 25, 1864

In Washington, D.C., in early December 1862, an aging German immigrant, an American president, the secretary of war, and a shabby, ill-mannered general known as "Old Brains" changed the rules of war forever. They had "no guide, no ground-work, no text book," but with "history, reason ... a sincere love of truth, justice and civilization," Columbia University law professor Francis Lieber labored to write a code of conduct for Union forces.[1]

Lieber was an innovator, a bred-in-the bone revolutionary, a humanitarian and a former soldier, born in Berlin on March 18, 1800. After fighting at Waterloo, Ligny and Namur, he was imprisoned for his political sentiments and published "songs of liberty."

Dr. Lieber's American journey began on February 17, 1832, when he became a citizen. His devotion to his adopted country and hatred of secession were well known, and his code was a first. "Nothing of the kind exists in any language," Lieber noted in a letter to Henry W. Halleck, general-in-chief of the U.S. army and military theoretician and lawyer.[2]

Lieber was right. After over a year of bloodshed, neither side had codified rules of conduct for officers in the field. And certainly, Confederate guerrillas termed "irregulars" or partisans rampaged and killed with impunity.

Thomas Pakenham, The Boer War (New York: Avon, 1979), p. 581.

Initially, the issue before Lieber was whether or how the Union should handle prisoners of war that were deemed guerrillas. The Confederates posed a great danger. "The rebel authorities claim the right to send men, in the garb of peaceful citizens, to waylay and attack our troops, to burn bridges and houses, and destroy property and persons within our lines," Halleck wrote to Lieber on August 6, 1862.[3]

Using "men in the garb of peaceful citizens" to attack and destroy defensively had become common practice among Southern ranks. Usually outnumbered on the battlefield, Confederate forces often relied on behind-the-lines guerrillas to weaken the enemy.

Halleck implored Lieber to define and codify such conduct:

> They [the Rebels] demand that such persons be treated as ordinary belligerents, and that when captured they extended to them the same rights as other prisoners of war; they also threaten that if such persons be punished as marauders and spies they will retaliate by executing our prisoners of war in their possession.[4]

Calling the subject of guerrilla (petty war) warfare "substantially a new topic in the law of war," Lieber wrote a lengthy essay defining unlawful bands of "brigands" as "evil doers in our civil war." He added "that no army, no society engaged in war, any more than a society at peace; can allow unpunished assassination, robbery, and devastation without the deepest injury to itself...."[5]

Vexing, to be sure, this issue of differentiating between a common criminal, a spy, and an irregular — a wolf in sheep's clothing. Lieber concluded that the law must treat robbers and their ilk as common criminals and that spies must be executed.

Abraham Lincoln was impressed. And Lieber, slight, aging, with sons on both sides of the conflict, was summoned to Washington.

"We gave Lieber leave of absence for a month," Columbia College trustee and diarist George Templeton Strong wrote on December 8, 1862, "the Secretary of War and General Halleck having telegraphed him to come to Washington at once. They want him to advise as a historical expert, either on military usages as to retaliation and other like questions," Strong added laconically, "or on some point of difference with foreign powers."[6]

While Lieber labored to fashion a framework for moral conduct in combat, his family, like his adopted country, was torn apart. "One of his three sons lost an arm at Fort Donelson," Strong reported. "Another, Oscar of South Carolina," was badly hit at Williamsburg, fighting in the ranks of the rebellion. His third son (Hamilton) was "reported much cut up in battle."[7]

In spite of Lieber's abolitionist sensibilities, the family spent years living in South Carolina when he was appointed to the chair of history and political economy at South Carolina College on June 5, 1835. With the position came "a salary of two thousand dollars a year and a house," an offer he could hardly refuse. But the decision was agony. "Oh, my poor life! ... I must bid farewell to all that is most precious and dear to me, and shall be compelled to live in

Professor Francis Lieber, author of *Law and Usages of War* (Library of Congress).

a Slave State," Lieber wrote. He added that he must support his family and would have "the time to write on subjects which have long occupied my mind."[8]

After 20 years in South Carolina, Lieber was elected to a similar position at Columbia College in New York City to embark on his treatise *Political Ethics,* "a study of the citizen in a democracy and his manifold relationship to his government," and his book *Civil Liberty and Self Government,* which stressed the unity of states as an organic entity not entitled to secession.[9]

Heartbroken by his son Oscar's decision to fight for the Confederacy and desperate to find another wounded son in the rows of dead and dying in the hospital, he wrote, "I knew war as [a] soldier, as a wounded man in the hospital, as an observing citizen. But I had yet to learn it in the phase of a father searching for his wounded son, walking through the hospitals, peering in the ambulances."[10]

Oscar Lieber, a prominent scientist and ardent Confederate, long estranged from his abolitionist father, did not survive his wounds. "Who is guilty of this Civil War, and what punishments do those on whom its guilt rests deserve?" Strong mused, adding that Lieber's tragedy was a "specimen of the practical effects of Civil War."[11]

The punishments and practical effects of war were very much on the mind of Abraham Lincoln when on April 24, 1863, he adopted and issued "General Orders No. 100," as Lieber's code would come to be known. It became the recognized standard for the laws of war and was followed until 1914, when it formed the basis for the Geneva Convention.

In June, Confederate leaders, in particular Secretary of War James A. Seddon, rejected General Orders No. 100, labeling it a hypocrisy, a whitewash of the problems written to give the federal government a moral high ground to commit atrocities. Seddon called the German professor and his code "a confused, unassorted [sic], and undiscriminating compilation," and went on to add that "a military commander under this code may pursue a line of conduct in accordance with principles of justice, faith, and honor, or he may justify conduct correspondent with the warfare of the barbarous hordes who overran the Roman Empire."[12]

If many in the South viewed the code as anathema, that belief was reinforced when invading Union forces under generals Sheridan, Hunter and Sherman, acting under discretionary permissions in section 15 of Lieber's code, reduced homes and cities to rubble. Section 15 read "Military necessity... allows of all destruction of life or limb of armed enemies and of other persons whose destruction is incidentally unavoidable in the armed contests of war ... it allows of all destruction of property ... and of all withholding of sustenance or means of life from the enemy...."

Even with guiding prohibitions included in Article 44 of Lieber's Code and its clear warnings stating that "All wanton violence committed against persons in the invaded country, all destruction of property not commanded by the authorized officer, all robbery, all pillage or sacking, even after taking a place by main force, all rape, wounding, maiming, or killing of such inhabitants, are prohibited under the penalty of death," the code left discretion up to the commanding officers, then as now.[13]

Article 56 stated "a prisoner of war is subject to no punishment for being a public enemy, nor is any revenge wreaked upon him by the intentional infliction of any suffering, or disgrace by cruel imprisonment, want of food, by mutilation, death, or any other barbarity." Article 44 protected the residents of an invaded land: "All wanton violence committed against persons in the invaded country, all destruction of property not commanded by the authorized officer, all robbery, all pillage or sacking … all rape, wounding, maiming or killing such inhabitants, are prohibited under penalty of death…. A soldier, officer or private, in the act of committing such violence, and disobeying a superior or ordering him to abstain from it, may be lawfully killed on the spot by such superior."

Certainly, General William T. Sherman's pledge to "make Georgia howl"[14] and the behavior of his marauding "Bummers" marching from Memphis to the sea are the subject of heated polemics to this day. But the invasion of the Southern states in rebellion against the Federal government was, in the eyes of the Union commanders and their president, a measure required to subjugate the Confederacy once and for all.

And because no one could have foreseen the mounting body counts and the endless winters and summers of horror, otherwise "humane" commanders took extreme measures. Admonished by Lieber to accord humanity to the enemy at all times, his code clearly stating that "Men who take up arms against one another in public war, do not cease on this account to be moral beings, responsible to one another, and to God,"[15] the actions and intentions of many supposedly governed by the same codes were called into question. And so, too, were their weapons.

Modern Civil War historians are challenged by seemingly ironclad presumptions about the lack of restraint and immoral conduct of some soldiers in the Civil War. There is no consensus, but there are surprises.

Military historian Mark Grimsley argues, "Although wanton depredations certainly occurred, I discovered almost no incidences in which white Southerners were killed, assaulted or raped." And, he adds, "My reading of the evidence did not sustain a portrayal of unrestrained destruction even of property."[16]

If, as Abraham Lincoln stated, soldiers are "thinking bayonets," the minds and hands of men behind the lines created new weapons with brains afire and deadly consequences.

Initially, both Northerners and Southerners considered new weapons of mass destruction. As early as January 1861, months before Confederate forces under General Pierre Beauregard fired the first volleys of the Civil War, South Carolina Governor Francis Pickens was urged to use exploding shells filled with arsenic and strychnine against the soldiers manning the federally controlled Fort Sumter. The letter's author, one John Condon residing in Jackson, Mississippi, proposed an "easy though desperate way to take Fort Sumter." He said that it "would make you and all other honorable men shudder," and went on to provide details: "My plan is this. During a heavy rain, throw bombshells charged or partly filled with strychnine or arsenic. They will explode scattering the poison all over the roof of the fort (which) supply the cisterns. The water will pass into them poisoning the whole concern–the effect you can imagine ... please burn this as soon as you read it."[17]

There is no record of a response from Pickens. Obviously, he did not destroy the letter, nor is there any record of his having authorized the use of John Condon's poison shells.

Assuredly and definitively, Lieber stated, "The use of poison in any manner, be it to poison wells or food or arms, is wholly excluded from modern warfare," adding, "He that uses it puts himself out of the pale of the law and usages of war."[18]

And later, with bravura, a New York schoolteacher, John Doughty, just 18 and a member of the 28th New York Light Artillery Regiment, devised a projectile shell containing chlorine gas. In a letter dated April 5, 1862, to Secretary of War Edwin M. Stanton, Doughty assured him that the Confederate's "first intimation of its presence would be by its inhalation ... rendering the disarming and capturing of them as certain as though both their legs were broken." Doughty enclosed a detailed diagram of the projectile and wrote, "Chlorine is a gas so irritating in its effects on the respiratory organs ... the men could not dodge it."

As to the moral question involved in the use of chlorine gas, he added, "I have, after watching the progress of events during the last eight months with reference to it, arrived at a somewhat paradoxical conclusion, that its introduction would very much lessen the sanguinary character of the battlefield, and at the same time render conflicts more decisive in their results. If I have erred, I have, *at least*, meant well."[19]

Either meaning well, still on the high ground, or not yet ready to engage such a measure, President Abraham Lincoln and his cabinet apparently refused to consider the proposal as there is again no record of the deployment of such a weapon.

There was more in the weapons arsenal that *was* endorsed by Abraham Lincoln: fire, specifically Greek fire. In ancient times, a column of flames was hurled from parapets, launched from ships at enemy fortifications.

This was a deadly, if erratic, weapon of war, probably made of phosphorous in a bisulphide of carbon. Its use did not end in ancient times, as many in the Civil War hailed the weapon which was prepared in vials, poured into shells, mixed in laboratories or carried in valises.

"Mr. Levi Short of the state of New York is the inventor of the article known as 'Solidified Greek fire,'" William B. Thomas wrote Abraham Lincoln on March 31, 1863. "I have written to him [Short] informing him of your desire to witness his experiments ... he will doubtless wait upon you in a very few days."[20]

Apparently Short had met Lincoln before. In January 1862 Lincoln witnessed two demonstrations of Short's "solidified Greek fire." In 1863, the shells were used in the bombardment of Vicksburg. Short also invented a liquid form of the Greek fire.

"The fire can neither be smothered out nor extinguished with water ... The first experiment made was with three and a half pints of liquid, which, upon being thrown into a barrel of water burned for seventeen and a half minutes ... the solidified was tried by throwing a quantity of it among a mass of chips and on a plank. The flame lasted over a minute and a quarter...." stated the *Scientific American* in 1863. "The experiments were witnessed by all the Navy yard officials, all of whom expressed great satisfaction at the trial." From all appearances, Greek fire was a precursor to napalm.[21]

Acting Rear Admiral David D. Porter, commander of the Mississippi squadron, extolled the virtues of the chemical in a letter of July 18, 1863, after the siege of Vicksburg. "I only had a small quantity, and used it against Vicksburg, setting the town on fire in three places in one night."[22]

Levi Short detailed the preparation: "First put the shell about a quarter of the bursting charge, then drop on top of the powder as many of the Greek fire cases as will easily slide down the inside of the shell. Your shell will be sure to fill its mission," he boasted.[23]

"There is a coal-black angel ... and he dwells (like the hunted and harried) in a swamp where the green frogs dip," wrote author Herman Melville upon hearing of the terror brought to the city of Charleston, South Carolina, on August 22, 1863, by a Greek fire-laden 16,700-pound Parrott cannon mounted on a parapet known as the "Swamp Angel." Melville continued, "But his face is against a City which is over the bay of the sea, and he breathes with a breath that is basement, and dooms by a far decree."

And of defiant Charleston having resisted Union artillery for two years, Melville wrote, "Is this the proud city? The scorner, which never would yield the ground? Which mocked the coal-black angel? The cup of despair goes round."[24]

The fire breathing "angel" of Melville's nightmare blew up a day later, a pile of harmless rubble, no longer a swamp creature, and was sold for scrap. The race to perfect the fire that armed the "swamp angel" spawned boasts and variations, ending only when Richmond fell to the North.

"I am in possession of a 'liquid fire,'" General Beauregard wrote in 1863, "which will make the Yanks open their eyes whenever I commence using it against their encampments."[25]

As the Confederacy's fierce resistance to Northern invaders grew more desperate, others in secret treasonous organizations in the North like the Sons of Liberty, in conjunction with clandestine operators and privateers, cooked, concocted and played with fire.

The 17th Missouri Infantry's Captain Richard Charles Bocking, a Dutch immigrant member of the Sons of Liberty, "in their employ and under their control" attempted to perfect Greek fire and shells "to be used by them [the Sons of Liberty] in their treasonable conspiracy and proposed insurrection." Entrepreneurial to a fault, former Union soldier Bocking had attempted to peddle his weapon to Union authorities.[26]

Unwilling to fight with Northern forces after the Emancipation Proclamation was announced, Bocking left the service and went to Louisville, Kentucky, to persuade the leaders of the Sons of Liberty to pay him for the conical shell filled with Greek fire contained in a "seemingly harmless portmanteau."

When an alarm clock "with the bell removed, set to any given time, springs the lock of a gun, the hammer of which, striking and exploding a cap, placed upon a tube filled with powder, fires a train connected with a bottle of Greek fire," the weapon would explode. Hunkered in the basement of a Louisville church on a Sunday morning and later in a hotel room, Bocking demonstrated the efficacy of his weapon. Impressed and eager for this time bomb, the Sons of Liberty (with Confederate Secret Service funds) representatives paid Bocking $200 immediately.[27]

Bocking's experiment was short-lived. It is probable that arson attacks on Louisville, Kentucky, wharves and warehouses were caused by Bocking's weapon. When Union detective and Sons of Liberty infiltrator Felix

Grundy Stidger testified against the treasonous group's leaders at the Indianapolis trials for treason, Bocking was deposed, arrested and imprisoned for one year.

Greek fire was still a seduction for the representatives of the Confederacy stationed in Canada. In late October 1864, Lieutenant Colonel Robert M. Martin, Lieutenant John William Headley, Captain Robert Cobb Kennedy and five other Confederate operatives were sent out of Canada on a mission to burn New York City to the ground. With handlers at the ready, these men, united by a common bond of hatred of Lincoln and his policies, nearly succeeded. With many wooden buildings, elegant hotels, tinderbox homes and restaurants crammed together, New York was an attractive target for men bent on the destruction of innocent civilians.

New York did not burn to the ground. Due in part to the ignorance, arrogance and haste of the arsonists who did not realize that oxygen was needed in order for the Greek fire to do major damage, the city was spared the worst. A better and more effective version was ordered.

By February 1865, a new version of Greek fire was perfected and tested by Columbia University professor Richard Sears McCulloh.

And in the North, as late as February 18, 1865, while his troops made ready to take Richmond, Ulysses S. Grant wrote to Major General Edward Ord, "If you have any shells filled with Greek Fire I wish you would experiment with a few of them on the abatis [fortification made of fallen trees] of the enemy and see if it can be set on fire."[28]

New weapons guaranteed to maim and kill had been introduced by 1863: percussion style torpedoes or subterra shells (land mines) and horological (time) bombs. Brigadier General Gabriel J. Rains of South Carolina, head of the Confederate Torpedo Bureau, invented the latter in early 1862.

In "old tidewater Virginia where spring comes early and beautifully,"[29] wrote historian Milton F. Perry, on an early May morning in 1862, an unearthly quiet was shattered when a soldier and his horse were blown to bits by an unseen foe. Just under the ground, tripped by hidden wires or exploded when stepped on, the landmine had come of age.

In 1864, Rains was granted permission to use land mines around Richmond, Mobile and Charleston.

"A thousand shells in battle are often thrown away, but here, every one counts, making its [the landmine's] work of destruction sure," he wrote in a recently discovered manuscript housed in the archives of the Museum of the Confederacy. The manuscript was initially examined by historian David Winfred Gaddy, and is reproduced in part for the first time by the present author.

Of interest and obvious importance is a portion of the large manuscript that concerns the use of land mines: "To stop Raiders — Let three men on swift horses ride after and round them, and plant small subterra shells in their route — or in some few miles around a city threatened, on the public roads leading thereto ... their destruction cannot be against the laws of God, when self-preservation is the law of nature."

Later in the manuscript, Rains defended the use of the deadly weapon:

> If we can cause the earth to open in a thousand places and destroy a host by fire and shells, soon no troops will be found to hazzard [sic] a march over such a volcano ... pure philanthropy led to this invention, for if by it we put a stop to all aggressive forays. Hostilities become impossible and when universally known, under the providence of God ... as wherein the dawn of that day when nations shall learn wars no more.[30]

The manuscript includes detailed instructions, drawings and usages of submarine mortar batteries and shells, vertical wood torpedoes, "dart grenades," torpedo boats, torpedo electric boats, "tin torpedoes" Demijohn torpedoes, copper torpedoes, and magnetic electric torpedoes. Electric primers as well as an incendiary bullet were "designated as a most infernal contrivance, to do evil, and is a thing not to be known among common people lest incendiarism [sic] fill the land with terror...."[31]

Exhilarated by his inventions, Rains contacted Jefferson Davis with regard to writing a memoir. Davis, worried that any printed document could never be kept secret, asked that he suppress the manuscript until after the war was over. According to John Coski of the Museum of the Confederacy in Richmond, Virginia, the manuscript in the museum's holdings is a reworking of the memoir Davis sought to suppress.

General William T. Sherman, outraged by reports of citizens and soldiers horribly mangled by General Rains' landmines, allegedly protested that the new weapon was not war, but murder. But in spite of the objections voiced by some on both sides of the conflict, Jefferson Davis kept a new explosive device on his desk as a souvenir. Supposedly, when Davis received a coal bomb, a "torpedo [explosive mine] covered with a mixture of broken coal and pitch & resemble pieces of Bituminous coal ... to be thrown into coal bins ... furnaces, etc." he called the device "perfection itself."[32]

After the fall of Richmond, Brigadier General Edward Hastings Ripley, commander at the occupation and capture of Richmond, found the coal bomb on Jefferson Davis' desk. "Intrigued by the device, Ripley sent it home to his father as a souvenir."[33]

By early 1864, despite gentlemen's codes and the destruction caused by landmines and coal bombs, more desperate measures were in play. A new kind of war, waged with inflammatory rhetoric and plans for mayhem, was raging in the Midwest in cities and towns allegedly loyal to the Union.

Largely forgotten in the body of Civil War literature is the story of a man who fought well. Felix Grundy Stidger was a government detective, to some a hero, to others a turncoat and informer. There was no starch, no strut for him as he went into the "devil's camp" to fight the destruction of the Union.

THREE

"When you go to fight the devil..."

"Who are the men that clamor most against the war, its cause and cost, and who Jeff Davis sometimes toasts? The Copperheads. ... And who will be the hiss and scorn of generations yet unborn, hated, despised, disgraced, forlorn? The Copperheads."

Author unknown

"A new danger looms up, larger and darker every day. It is nothing less than civil war in the Northwest States! They are honeycombed by secret societies, working in aid of the rebellion, and controlled by reckless, desperate traitors for whom the gallows is far too good."

George Templeton Strong,
September 6, 1864*

"When you go to fight the devil, go into his camp with fire and do not be afraid of being burnt."

Detective Felix Grundy Stidger†

"He ruined us all," Confederate agent Thomas Henry Hines allegedly said of Union counterspy Felix Grundy Stidger. "He ruined us all."[1]

Between May and September of 1864, the dry goods clerk turned government informant infiltrated the seditious order known as the Sons of Liberty and allowed federal authorities to seize the chief conspirators and bring the secret order to an end. "I said it would have succeeded but for the traitor in the camp," Thomas Hines wrote, bemoaning the demise of a prized Confederate plot. "'Twas well planned."[2]

*Allan Nevins and Milton Halsey Thomas, eds. The Diary of George Templeton Strong. Vol. 3: The Civil War. (New York: Macmillan, 1952), p. 482.
†Felix G. Stidger, Treason History of the Sons of Liberty (Chicago: Felix Stidger, 1903), p. 10.

26

The "traitor in the camp" was an accidental hero, wily, uncommonly brave and extremely lucky. Always endangered, usually outnumbered, Felix Stidger survived his mission, leaving "unimpeachable evidence of his counter-espionage for the Union."[3]

And if many of Stidger's enemies wanted him dead, his government was grateful. "It is to the rare fidelity of this man...the government has been chiefly indebted for the exposure and designs of the conspirators...." Judge Advocate General Joseph Holt wrote to Secretary of War Stanton when summarizing the "intensely treasonable and revolutionary spirit" of secret organizations that had rapidly expanded throughout the war.[4]

Felix Grundy Stidger, United States government secret service agent, 1864 (Chicago Historical Society).

The purpose of the Sons of Liberty was threefold according to Brigadier General Henry Beebee Carrington, commander of the military district of Indiana at Indianapolis and a fervent Copperhead foe: "To prevent a four year succession of the war party, to force a recognition of the Southern Confederacy's freedom ... to resist all military process and to prevent the reelection of the present government ... if necessary by force."[5]

Earlier espionage efforts had revealed their "entire machinery, resulting in the arrest, conviction and punishment through the United States Courts of 150 persons."[6] It was not enough.

After the battles of Gettysburg and Vicksburg, the Sons of Liberty had plans to effect the release of 40,000 Confederate prisoners held at Camp Douglas in Chicago and in other northern cities. Anticipating mayhem and planning conflagrations and armed uprisings, Illinois, Missouri, Indiana, Ohio and parts of Kentucky would be delivered to the Confederacy.

So secret were the movements and so strong the forces of the Sons of Liberty that the federal government was at a loss as to how to stop it.

The Sons were the latest incarnation in a sprawl of secret organizations that "had for its sole object the dissolution of the Union and the establishment of Southern Empire." The Knights of the Golden Circle counted among its members "nearly every man of influence in the south (and many a pretended Union man in the north)" at least three decades before the Civil War."[7]

An eccentric physician of dubious credentials, Dr. George William Lamb Bickley, called a "magnificent charlatan" by historian James O. Hall and a "wonderful old humbug" by author James D. Horan, was father to and founder of the Knights of the Golden Circle, the most famous of these fraternal orders. Aptly described as a "Southern fire-eater," Bickley endorsed the idea of expanding the institution of slavery into southern Mexico by seizing the whole country. The notion of colonization and expansion excited many southerners, but Bickley and his followers took it a step beyond diplomacy. With the vision of new lands and more slaves, the Knights organized their first "castles," or cells, in Cincinnati, Ohio, and fast spread south, their theories and grandiose plans were music to the ears of plantation gentry and anti-administration secessionists.

By 1860, Bickley's outsized and half-cocked persona proved too much for his followers. When a vote of no confidence sealed his fate, he denied any failure and claimed his departure from the Knights was voluntary. Historian G.F. Milton disagreed, calling Bickley "as untrustworthy as he was romantic."

When the Civil War began, the Knights turned from their Mexican cabal to the Confederacy. Espousing secession was not enough, a new revolution had begun and needed to establish roots in the North, particularly in border states where conflicts raged and confederate sentiments abounded.

In 1863, the Knights of the Golden Circle was "reorganized as the Order of American Knights and again, in early 1864, as the Order of the Sons of Liberty with Ohio Democratic congressman Clement Vallandigham, most prominent of the Copperheads, as its supreme commander."[8]

His anti–Lincoln, pro–Copperhead views were well known both in Ohio and New York. Labeled by Carl Sandburg as "a peace man of shaded sincerity," Vallandigham's cries for cooperation with the South at any cost, even if it meant leaving the institution of slavery intact, angered many in the Lincoln administration. But his defeat in the 1862 Congressional election did little to silence his inflammatory rhetoric. In May 1863, after making a speech calling "King" Lincoln's war "wicked, cruel and necessary," Vallandigham was arrested and charged with violating General Order No. 38, a government proclamation that established the death penalty for specific acts of treason and a zero tolerance for sympathy with the Confederate cause in speech as well as deed. When a military commission found Vallandigham guilty, he was imprisoned. The hue and cry that followed challenged the President to reconsider Vallandigham's punishment. Lincoln sent Vallandigham behind the lines and into the Confederacy. Gone but not forgotten, Vallandigham was nominated for governor of Ohio in absentia. When he returned to his native state he was not re-arrested. He died on June 17, 1871, in a bizarre courtroom accident after shooting himself with a gun he was using to demonstrate the circumstances of a murder. If the Vallandigham case demonstrated that the arrest violated the rights of speech of a U.S. citizen, thousands of other seditious Americans were not intimidated.

And by early April 1864, the "fire in the rear" that had so worried President Lincoln seemed inextinguishable. Further intelligence revealed serious Confederate support and funding; hundreds of thousands of dollars and the promise of an additional ten percent of the value of all things destroyed to the saboteurs. New members were being recruited in large numbers, especially in Kentucky and Indiana.

"While the government knew of the existence of this treasonable organization and had kept track of the changes of names … Circle of Honor, going to the Knights of the Golden Circle, later to the Order of American Knights and finally on February 22, 1864, to the Order of the Sons of Liberty," Felix Stidger wrote in his late-in-life tell-all *Treason History of the Sons of Liberty* that no agent to date had infiltrated the highest ranks of the secret orders or had, as Stidger said, "engaged in the practice of revealing the designs of this treasonable organization with the express purpose of giving information to the government, and saving bloodshed, and possibly national disaster."[9]

Two months later, based on Stidger's information, Carrington warned Captain C.H. Potter, Assistant Adjutant General in Columbus, Ohio: "The existence of the organization [The Sons of Liberty] is a fact … their leaders are surely endeavoring to educate their people to the contingency of actual war."[10]

In Stidger's words: "There is an old adage, that 'forewarned is fore-armed,' and in this instance the saving of the United States government lay almost wholly in the fact of the government officials being fully fore-warned and ready to meet these conspirators in any move they would make...."[11]

And forewarn he did, but with a sense of foreboding. "They speak of murder," he wrote in one of many breathless, explicit communications. And later, he wrote, "I can't trust anyone any more ... assassination awaits me on the least suspicion."[12]

In fact, assassination "awaited" Stidger to the end of his life. Years later, old, homesick and infirm, hundreds of miles from the bluegrass state of his childhood, Stidger remembered simple things: the wheeze of the calliope from the levee on the Ohio, the perfume of a Kentucky sum-mer. But of his mission, one of the most dangerous ever asked of a Civil War spy, Stidger wrote, "When you go to fight the devil, go into his camp with fire, and do not be afraid of being burnt."[13]

If his biography, excepting his "one good story" as his obituary stated, gives facts unremarkable, it does hint at something other than self-glorification. And if his double life was incited by an incident sad and preventable, his early hardscrabble years of poverty and home schooling were marked by a hunger to learn and an unending devotion to his wid-owed mother.

Felix Grundy Stidger was born in Taylorsville, Kentucky, a tiny ham-let set in the undulate bluegrass hills 35 miles northwest of Louisville, on August 5, 1836, to Harman A. Stidger, a carpenter, and Narcissa Holsclaw, a farmer's daughter. Harman Stidger died in 1838 when Felix was two years old and his brother John was an infant. He was home schooled by his mother until the age of eight, his formal education erratic at best. "In those days in Kentucky," he wrote, "there was no such advan-tage as a free school."[14]

He went to class in winter, worked on the farm in summer and fall; that was the drill until he was 12. He struggled to learn anything, verses and numbers, always, numbers. The Stidgers were an ordinary, poor fam-ily with two hungry boys. Narcissa sewed for neighbors when she could, and the oldest child, Felix, feared for them all.

In 1850, according to the Spencer County census, Taylorsville was composed of saddlers, millers, blacksmiths, one innkeeper, two "idiots," one "insane" man, a schoolteacher and a constable. With their property

You Do Not Know the Great Peril

The Armies At The Front Were in Danger of From a Powerful Secret Enemy in the Rear in the Summer and Fall of 1864.

YOU CAN GET THE FULL HISTORY OF IT FROM THIS BOOK.

FELIX G. STIDGER,

Company E, 15th Regiment Kentucky Volunteer Infantry. Service in the Office of the Assistant Adjutant General, 1st Division, 14th Army Corps, Department of the Cumberland. Leaving Army in 1864, become U. S. Govt. Secret Service Agent, And Grand Secretary of State Order of Sons of Liberty for the State of Kentucky May, 1864; Principal Witness for the U. S. Government in the trials of the Conspirators for Treason in Indianapolis in 1864; And the Breaker Up of the Knights of the Golden Circle or Order of Sons of Liberty in the States of Indiana, Kentucky, Illinois, and Ohio.

Dear Sir and Comrade:

I send you herewith a sample page, though on thinner paper, of a History that I have just issued of facts that have never before been published. Those that knew of my work in this Treasonable organization have for years desired me to publish a History of my Personal Experiences while Grand Secretary for the State of Kentucky of the Order of Sons of Liberty, or Knights of the Golden Circle, in 1864, as there has never been an authentic publication on the designs and secret workings and intentions of that Order.

This volume contains the Secret Work of that Order; its signs, grips, pass-words, etc., through the Five Degrees of the Order, from the lowest degree up to and including the Grand Council Degree, and have never before been published. It also contains the True History of the Designs and Intentions of the Leaders of that Order, how they were to be carried into execution; and how the United States Government was kept as Fully Informed of their intentions as the leaders themselves were; as I was the only man in the Employ of the United States Government that ever obtained all the Degrees of the Order and a High Officer in the Order.

The book is printed on heavy paper, and substantially bound in cloth. It contains Historical Facts that have never before been for himself, and place in the hands of his children that they may learn the peril in which their father at the front, and the Government were placed in 1864, and of which the Government itself was ignorant until this information now published was obtained.

Knowing, as I do, the difficulty of getting a good attendance of members at the regular meetings of the Posts I know you will find a copy of this History of such attraction as to induce a full attendance at every meeting of your Post by having the Adjutant of your Post read a few pages every meeting to the members present, and they would from the first become sufficiently interested as to attend regularly, and inform other members of the interest in attending.

Hon. H. S. Boutell, M. C., 6th Congressional District, says: "I have examined your book with interest." February 10th, 1904.

If you should not feel willing to incur the whole expense of a copy of the book for your Post you can readily induce other members or friends to share the expense with you, and reduce the expense to 10 or 15 cents each, and let the book become the property of the Post instead of an individual member.

Where the Post, or friends, wish to club together and obtain one dozen copies, or more, in one order, I furnish them, and I pay the express charges, on receipt of $12.00 for one dozen copies, and $1.00 per copy for as many over one dozen as desired. Single copies sent, postage paid, on receipt of $1.50, money order or registered letter. Hoping that you may find it of interest to you to send for one or more copies, I am, Fraternally yours,

FELIX G. STIDGER, 559 Orleans Street, CHICAGO.

KNIGHTS OF THE GOLDEN CIRCLE,

Treason History,

Order of Sons of Liberty,

A Treasonable Organization in the North,

CIVIL WAR OF 1861-1865.

Promotional flyer for Stidger's book (courtesy of Nancy Clayton).

valued at $400, 45-year-old Narcissa, 13-year-old Felix and 12-year-old John were wedged, absent a head of household, between the large broods of the Boston and Simms families.

At 15, with the equivalent of only three years of schooling, Stidger "was placed in the office of the County Clerk ... where [he] picked up a smattering of the law, as well as becoming thoroughly familiar with the duties...."[15]

Unable to support his mother on meager earnings while he waited for advancement, Stidger went to work carrying mortar for a plasterer at 25 cents a day. Apprenticed two years later to a carpenter, Stidger, with an obvious bent for facts and numbers, also kept the carpenter's books. When his employer bought an interest in a dry goods store in the town of Fairfield, Stidger followed. But ever restive and hungry for money, Stidger was back to carpentering after two years.

In 1860, Stidger was off again, to Bloomfield, Kentucky, hoping to make more money working as a clerk for his former employer. A bucolic spot that lacked both a telegraph and a railroad station, "the town of Bloomfield was a very pretty little place with an intelligent population, a well to do surrounding county and withal an infernally disloyal sentiment against the United States government ... a town of rebel insults and rebel yells," he wrote.[16]

By 1861, as Stidger toiled away at "merchant tailoring," seven states had seceded from the Union. In fact, Stidger related, Bloomfield contained just four union sympathizers. "After the election in November," he wrote, "the feelings and expressions of hatred against the North knew no bounds in that little town, in fact it could not have been more intense in Charleston, South Carolina ... it was considered that I ought not to be so free with expressions of loyalty to the United States government, all of which made me more out-spoken and offensive in my expressions against disloyalty, rebellion and treason."[17]

Armed with a fervent belief in the Union and a ready, good gun, Stidger stayed on in Bloomfield. "While I remained in the town some eight months afterward ... it became so that I never went to or came from my meals without having slurs, insults and insinuations hurled at me." Forced to use back alleys facing buildings that might conceal him, he stayed alive. He commented dryly, "They all knew that I carried a Colts Navy and a dirk knife."[18]

Late in April 1862, Stidger returned to Taylorsville with the prospect of a new construction job. Hammer in hand, ever anxious to provide for his impoverished mother, Stidger had managed to sit out the war thus far. In September, that would all change. Confederate General Braxton Bragg's forces, in an effort to "free Kentucky," invaded the state, blazing their way through Taylorsville until they retreated toward Perryville, unable to stop Union General Don Carlos Buell's advance.[19]

"General Rousseau and First Lieutenant William P. McDowell," Stidger said, "expressed a wish that some loyal young man of the town should join in the ranks of the army, when he would be at once detailed as a clerk in the Assistant Adjutant General's Office at division headquarters, whereupon I applied for and obtained the position."[20]

Two days later, he followed the command to the little town of Sharpsville. "On the next morning, October 8th, I found the division already moving ... I witnessed and partly participated in one of the hardest fought battles for the length of time and the number of men engaged that was fought during the war."[21]

The battle that thrust the tiny village of Perryville into the thick of war was one of the bloodiest. Fought in the rolling bluegrass terrain, through streams and swamps, and in the town itself, over 7,500 men were killed in a "battle [that] was as decisive as any other during the entire four year conflict, for it marked a fatal loss of initiative for the South."[22]

Confederate General Braxton Bragg noted the cost of the swift pitched battle. "For the time engaged the severest and most desperately contested fighting within my knowledge."[23]

Stidger's take was more visceral. "I never saw dead men lay so thick," he wrote, "as the rebels on the battlefield of Perryville after the Union dead had all been buried." Not even his presence at the battle of Stone River and Chickamauga scalded his senses in quite the same way.[24]

Just after the battle of Perryville, in a random act of generosity that was to be his entrée into the Sons of Liberty, Stidger gave his precious horse to Union major Henry Kalfus, later a traitor to the United States and a leader of the group. Kalfus wanted out of the Union army; he'd tried with no success to tender his resignation twice before with no luck. He was not alone in his sentiments. Many Union soldiers switched sides early in the war, and over half the ranks of the 15th Kentucky had been killed in a matter of weeks.

The third time Kalfus tried to leave the Union ranks, according to

Stidger, he alleged "as his reason for so doing that he had entered the army for the purpose of assisting in the suppression of the rebellion, but since the consummation of the Proclamation of President Lincoln for the freeing of the slaves of the South, he declined to further participate in a war of which the ultimate result was to be the freedom of the Negro." He was put under arrest. Stidger relates the circumstances: "The 15th Regiment Kentucky Infantry be drawn up in line, that Major Kalfus be brought under guard ... his shoulder straps cut off."[25]

The punishment continued. Kalfus was dishonorably discharged in front of the entire regiment, after which he was "marched outside the lines of the army at the point of a bayonet...." Kalfus would go back to Kentucky and plunge deeply into the cabals of the Sons of Liberty, determined to fight the Union on his terms.[26]

"There seemed to be a species of hydrophobic mania strike the Officers of the 15th Kentucky Infantry to resign," Stidger related. And he too was conflicted. "During the winter of 1863 and sixty-four my mother was confined to her bed ... and wanted me to come home on a furlough."[27] Knowing he could expect leave of no more than ninety days, he wrote, "If I should have to leave here at the point of death it would be worse that not to go home ... about the 10th of February, 1864, I determined to pursue my discharge from the army."[28]

The request for a discharge on medical grounds was summarily denied. With a good bit of wheedling, and perhaps a dose of chicanery, Stidger managed to obtain a discharge form from the camp surgeon: "When coming to the part where it was necessary for him to fill in the nature of my complaint ... I readily inserted 'a predisposition to consumption, hereditary in its character' and passed the paper back for his signature." He left Chattanooga "for home that evening."[29]

Home by then was frequently terrorized by Confederate guerrillas that "took advantage of every occasion to mistreat and rob union citizens." The Stidgers were high on their list. On a trip to fill a prescription for his mother, Stidger "took a large pocketbook from ... inside my vest, from which I took the money to pay for a prescription," in full view of people "I knew personally and well, everyone in the store, as I had been raised with them."[30]

That night marauding thugs invaded his home. Stidger and his brother were robbed at gunpoint in full view of his mother as she lay dying. One week later, "her death most certainly hastened by the appearance of those craven cowards," Stidger swore to his mother that he would not kill the invaders. Instead, he would try to expose them. In the small village, surrounded by enemies, a bad situation got worse. Stidger and his brother were stalked by a band of assassins hired by a neighbor. Stidger escaped by fleeing to Louisville. "Our friends learned of the fact and hid my brother for the night, and the next day he also came to Louisville."[31]

Intent on "evening up the score with the guerrillas, their sympathizers and abettors," Stidger decided to apply for a job "in the United States Government Secret Service Force." Initially rebuffed, he tried again and again, finding "promises only." Determined to report disloyalty to the government, since arriving in Louisville Stidger had been "interviewing" and covertly gathering information from Confederate sympathizers in the town, which by now, as the rest of Kentucky, was under martial law.[32]

Armed with more than just rumor and expecting no compensation, Stidger managed to convey his dispatches to Stephen P. Jones, provost Martial General office for the Military District of Kentucky. If Jones regarded the first few letters with "some skepticism, deeming their revelations the result of either romantic writing or blind luck," that was to change.[33]

Jones had received a letter from General Carrington, Stidger relates. "I learned that Doctor William A. Bowles, the owner of French Lick Springs in Indiana (the military head of the Kentucky based order)... one of the leaders of a treasonable organization known as "The Sons of Liberty"... was in a few days going into the state of Kentucky to organize lodges of that treasonable organization." Carrington was looking for a "reliable Kentuckian for special and extra hazardous duty in Kentucky." When Jones asked Stidger if he could help, Stidger leapt at the opportunity, with a caveat.

"I told him that if Doctor Bowles went into a part of the state where I was known I could not [help] but if he went where I was not known, I thought I could." Jones told Stidger he had a month. If he failed, all bets were off. He was immediately ordered to French Lick Springs to find and gain the confidence of the fanatical and notorious "Doc" Bowles, a wealthy Indiana physician and property owner who touted the "miraculous and healing waters" of his French Lick Springs hotel and cure-all spa.[34]

Before Stidger left on his mission, he was briefed on the scant knowledge the government had on the secrets of Sons of Liberty. A quick course on hand signals, grips, codes and pledges of "the Vestibule, or Neophyte Degree ... that being all that was in the possession of any member of the government," followed.[35]

Later, after he had successfully climbed to the highest levels of the Sons, he would recount them in detail to a stunned courtroom. While it was clear that uprisings and mayhem were plotted at the higher vestibule levels, even members of the lower orders worried Union officials. "The members of the lower degree are often for a considerable period kept quite unaware of the true purposes of their chiefs, ... but are bound to yield prompt and implicit obedience to the utmost of their ability, without remonstrance, hesitation or delay."[36]

If Stidger could successfully infiltrate the Sons, Jones reasoned, there was a chance to stop them before they could act. When could he go to Indiana, Jones asked, how soon could he begin? Without hesitation Stidger stated, "I at once set upon for preparing myself ... for a duty I knew nothing about ... procured a set of common, gray [butternut] clothing ... and a pair of spectacles...." With little more than borrowed rebel garb, a jumble of pledges racing through his brain and a fortuitous case of mistaken identity, Stidger set off for French Lick Springs. At once, he bluffed his way into the good graces of Bowles' gatekeeper, Horace Heffren. Overjoyed at the arrival of the efficient, somber Stidger, Heffren mistook him for a "long awaited messenger" from Bowles. Stidger assured him he was indeed the man. Heffren, like Kalfus, was a deserter from the Union army, sworn to uphold the secrets of the order. He was a politician, a democratic representative in the Indiana legislature, described by a political adversary as "a disgusting compound of whiskey, grease, vulgarity and cowardice." Stidger's first dispatch to Jones on May 13 rings with pride at his lucky break. His impression of Bowles was immediate and penetrating: "I knew him at once to be a man that would engage in secret scheming.... He has one of the worst countenances I ever saw a man have. He cannot look anyone in the face one minute, I believe. His head and general appearance would indicate great cunning and the exercise of any underhanded move to carry that cunning into execution, but he will not face anything equally and boldly."[37]

At first, Stidger used his own name in his communications. Later, afraid of blowing his cover, he altered his handwriting and used the alias "J.J. Eustis" and hid the reports in all manner of boxes, containers and makeshift mailboxes. Sometimes his brother John took them into headquarters, posing as an innocent courier. Whatever the nature of the delivery, the government deemed Stidger's information invaluable: "Heffren told me that he was daily expecting a commissioner from some rebel forces then disbanded in Kentucky for the purposes of co-operating with the sons of Liberty ... when they should be sufficiently organized in ... Kentucky, Indiana, Illinois, Missouri and Ohio to liberate the rebel prisoners...." Many men were at the ready, Heffren told Stidger, and waiting for a call to arms.[38]

With Heffren's endorsement, Stidger was off to French Lick Springs and a meeting with Dr. Bowles. Once Stidger had assured him he had taken the Second Vestibule degree (remarkably, Bowles didn't question him), Bowles revealed the "perfect understanding with the Confederate forces" and the promise of 60,000 turncoat troops. Arming them was a problem, but, Bowles told Stidger, they were working on it.

"He told me that I was then surrounded with members of the Order; and that he was military chief ... for the state of Indiana.... The forces of Indiana and Ohio would concentrate in Kentucky, and make Kentucky their battleground ... the forces of Illinois would proceed to St. Louis, and cooperate with those of Missouri; that Illinois would furnish 50,000 men ... Missouri, 30,000 men, and that the rebel General Sterling Price would invade Missouri with 30,000 troops," Stidger wrote. Moreover, other Confederate generals under orders would send additional troops. "I remained at Dr. Bowles' four days and returned to Louisville," Stidger added.[39]

After turning in a six-page written report, "Which I did entirely from memory, as I considered it injudicious to make any notes," Stidger turned to his old friend Dr. Henry Kalfus, by then firmly ensconced in the Sons of Liberty:

"I called on him and renewed our old acquaintance ... informing him that I had procured my discharge from the army of the United States, and that I had 'seen the elephant and he had horns' [an expression known to indicate a disloyal sentiment to the Union]... and that I wanted nothing more to do with the United States Army, and intimated to him that I had an intention of becoming a member of an organization that was opposed to suppression of the rebellion and freedom for the Negro...."[40]

After assuring Kalfus that he had taken degrees in the Sons of Liberty, and solemnly reciting vows of the order ("The government designated the United States of America has no sovereignty ... resistance by force of arms is not revolution but assertion of right ... I do solemnly swear that I will obey at all times, without question, all rightful commands of the order") Stidger won Kalfus' complete confidence. "Kalfus urged upon me to make his office my headquarters when in the city."[41]

Bluff and blarney carried Stidger from post to post, and the authorities were compiling a complete dossier of names he was so meticulously reporting. Convinced by now of Stidger's prowess as a spy, Colonel Carrington fed his information to Captain C.H. Potter, the assistant Adjutant General of Ohio. "There is a Supreme Grand Council, with both Civil and Military Organization ... [and] they have commissioned four major-generals for Indiana ... while other portions occupy Louisville and Kentucky. The senior major-general is William A. Bowles ... the others are Yagel, Humphreys and Milligan — all rank blasphemers of the government."[42]

Of Stidger, Carrington wrote, "One of the high officials of the order left this city this morning with the cipher, seal and private books required for use there. He came here with an order to have out of the way [assassinated] Detective Coffin ... and Judge Bullitt furnished money for the trip." Carrington asked for money — "$10,000, or even $5,000" — to aid in Stidger's missions. Fear of losing his best spy was not groundless.[43]

"During the three months that I had my headquarters ... in the office of ex–Major Doctor Henry F. Kalfus, were I away from Louisville even for a day or more, on my return I was ... in the greatest fear of death ... knowing ... the unreasoning desperation of the men whom I would meet there," Stidger wrote. "If they found anything ... of my actual work for the government ... I would be shot down and killed instantly...." Because spies usually wore civilian dress and moved through the enemy as one of their own, by law, Stidger faced execution if exposed.[44]

His return to Bowles at French Lick revealed a stunner from Richmond: "[Jefferson] Davis agrees to send Buckner or Breckenridge, or even Longstreet, if they ask into Kentucky...." Accompanying Bowles to further meetings, Stidger learned of the failure of Greek fire as a tool of sabotage and of a new version perfected by chemist Charles Bocking. On a Sunday afternoon, in the basement of a Louisville church, Stidger witnessed the demonstration of Bocking's fire. "It is a liquid," Stidger said, "and can be carried in a vial." Increasingly reliant on Stidger, Bowles sent him to Judge Joshua F. Bullitt, a prominent Louisville attorney and head of the Kentucky Council. Bullitt, Stidger reported, "was willing to spend the last damn dollar he had in this organization, for he hoped to soon be able to steal a good living from the damned sons of bitches, meaning the Union...."[45]

With Bullitt believing he had a ready helper, one who was brilliant with numbers and a keeper of secrets, Stidger advanced quickly. "In Louisville, he actually took the second degree oath. Now he was ready to be admitted into the secret councils," wrote historian James D. Horan. And, remarkably, he was[46]:

> Captain ... I am to be Secretary of the grand Council of this State. You shall know everything, but I ask of you to let as few as possible, or no one, know where you get your information.... So have no one arrested on my reports ... set other men on the track ... and let them give the evidence.... Assassination awaits me on the least suspicion.[47]

"Nor was this an idle fear," wrote historian G.F. Milton. As Secretary to the Grand Council, Stidger heard and recorded it all:

> In caucus it is decided that we cannot organize a Grand Council until Mr. Coffin [a union detective] is killed ... I go tomorrow to Dr. Bowles to have the work carried into execution, of hunting him up and having him killed. I go from there to Indianapolis to H.H. Dodd on the same business. Can you not try and get word to Mr. Coffin in some way.... To hear the way those men talk about murdering Coffin is sufficient to make me guarded.[48]

When no word came from Carrington, Stidger raced through the night to deliver the dispatch and above all, to warn Coffin, a man he'd never met. Not able to immediately find him, Stidger kept an appointed rendezvous with cell leaders Harrison H. Dodd, the Grand Commander of the Order of American Knights, William Bowles, and lawyer Lambdin Milligan. Intent on killing the improbably named Coffin, the leaders ordered more men to find him and execute him on the spot. Stidger proposed that he himself track Coffin and make the kill.

The man readily agreed and Stidger was given $25 to fulfill the contract. He dashed through alleyways until he was able to deliver the news of Coffin's immediate peril to his Union commander's office. Immediately, Coffin was snatched from a train and removed from the field, but Stidger himself was in grave danger. One of Bowles' assistants was suspicious and perhaps jealous of the alert brought by the diligent new man. "Do not," Stidger again begged Carrington, "tell anyone what work I am doing.... I shall be betrayed and murdered in my sleep." A defiant Bowles confronted his aide and vouched for Stidger. Stidger was safe for the moment, but he lived in constant fear of exposure.[49]

"My only safety now is in entire secrecy," he added, deliberately leaving his dispatch unsigned.[50] "There were but five persons that knew the actual business in which I was engaged. First of these was Miss Josephine M. McGill of Louisville ... to whom I was engaged to be married, and although every one of her family were the bitterest enemies of the government I fully advised her of every move I made, and everything I did ... which confidence she proved herself worthy...." The others were his brother John, Captain Jones, Colonel Thomas B. Farleigh, and his government appointed assistant, James Prentice.[51]

With Coffin safe, Stidger sounded a new alarm. "They want to get ready for action while the Federal forces are out of Kentucky, at the front ... they consider Kentucky now fully ripe." A major uprising was planned for July 4. Men and arms were flowing into the state.[52]

On June 17, the day he received Stidger's information, Carrington sent an urgent warning to Secretary of War Stanton. "This matter is worthy the grave consideration of the President, his cabinet, and the general-in-chief, and that the contingency of grave domestic issues is possible."[53] His spy was proving indispensable. Stidger was one step ahead of the enemy and the government was anxious to move in. Now Carrington had to pray he stayed alive. "Stidger is ... accepted as the only safe man in that state [Kentucky] for these traitors to negotiate with," Carrington wrote to Captain C.H. Potter. "Having due notice of their plans, I expect to anticipate them; but it will not do to ignore them. The leaders of the order are desperate men. They have little to lose, all to gain by disorder."[54]

Safe, perhaps in Carrington's view, but hardly in Stidger's. "Some suspicion has been cast upon me here by someone," he wrote, "but I was gallantly defended by Judge Bullitt...." With each visit to Indianapolis, Stidger found a way to see Carrington. Things were coming to a head. "Already the two had cooked up plans for a final pounce," wrote G.F. Milton. But timing, according to Stidger, was key.

Stidger wrote to Carrington outlining a strategy, delaying the arrests, buying time. "When I saw you in Indianapolis, you mentioned something about your taking possession of the building where the books of the Council are kept. If such a step is not absolutely necessary before the first of September, the propriety of putting it off until about that time is plain."[56]

Apparently, the "quarterly reports of the county temples" would not be issued again until the first of August. By waiting, Stidger reasoned, more incriminating evidence could be seized all at once.

Events moved rapidly. Stidger urged his superiors to arrest Captain Bocking immediately. The chemist's volatile Greek fire weaponry was being readied for use in the upcoming insurrection. According to Stidger, a Confederate spy had been present at the Greek fire demonstration and "was leaving with samples to carry them through the lines to the Southern ordnance experts, for their possible manufacture."[57]

Stidger's advice was ignored. "They are preparing for action," he warned. "The leaders are so anxious that I would not be surprised at hostilities commencing in this state before the third of August."[58]

Mercifully, the Sons delayed. Coordination was proving difficult for a tri-state massing of weapons and men. Hour by hour, Stidger compiled membership lists for delivery to his new Louisville sub-chief, Lieutenant Thomas Farleigh. He reported, "By name all prominent members of the county, also the number and kinds of arms and amount of ammunition of every form."[59]

From his catbird's seat in the group's many meetings, Stidger also revealed a plot to destroy a train carrying Negro troops to Nashville over the Louisville Railroad. "I reported this fact to Colonel Farleigh within an hour after I received the information."[60]

A few days later, Stidger learned that the same train had been sent out, "but instead of carrying Negro soldiers it had carried one or two flat cars well supplied with artillery, and that the Negro troops had been sent by steamboats." The saboteurs watched as the train slowed and then shelled the area. They scattered, making a frantic escape. The cell leaders were outraged that the government had been alerted. Stidger wrote that he "sympathized" with them and "expressed great regret that they had been thwarted in their plans."[61]

Stidger swore that "The members of the order in Illinois were to concentrate at Chicago and Rock Island and release the rebel prisoners ... they were then to seize the arsenals at those places and arm the released prisoners. The three divisions in Illinois were to seize the railroads and form forces with Jefferson Davis' 20,000 men from Missouri." Blood would run in the streets and the North would be thrown into chaos with the funding and blessing of the Rebel government.[62]

In Indianapolis, Stidger, Governor Oliver P. Morton, Major General

Alan P. Hovey, Farleigh and Carrington huddled. Plans were made for a final search and seizure operation with Stidger supplying locations of documents, ammunition and the secret locations of the leaders. Perhaps, with the end so near, Stidger couldn't bear to break the news in person. He wrote a letter, a bombshell. "I deem it my duty," he told Carrington, "to give you timely notice that I shall have to give up my present employment on the first of September." It seemed that Stidger's beloved fiancé, Josephine McGill, had grown increasingly concerned for his safety. "On or about that time [September 1]," Stidger continued, "I form an alliance with one whose happiness I deem it my duty to do all in my power to protect ... you will please determine how I am to be enabled to quit without suspicion."[63]

And, Stidger added, should the Sons be arrested, testifying against them might well cost him his life. "If I am furnished with a sufficiency to live hereafter in protection," he wrote, he might be willing. In reality, Stidger knew this was a nearly impossible request. It appeared that Carrington's great spy was slipping away.[64]

Stidger would have known that one vital piece of evidence was missing, an irrefutable link between the Confederate government and the Sons. Dodd had gone back and forth to Canada with other members of the Sons to insure Confederate funds and cooperation in their plans, not the least of which would be an attempt to assassinate Oliver P. Morton, the anti–Copperhead governor of Indiana. Moreover, Judge Bullitt had just returned from Canada where he had been given $10,000 in checks signed by Jacob Thompson and $5,000 in gold, a direct and legally irrefutable connection, the "indisputable evidence of his treasonous dealings."[65]

One last mission remained. "I worked my brain most vigorously the entire time ... trying to form some way for having Bullitt arrested," Stidger wrote, "for I MUST have it done at any hazard."[66] With Bullitt out of the way, Dodd would be forced to rely exclusively on Stidger to convey information throughout Kentucky and Indiana. Stidger arranged to meet him at the Louisville ferry. As Carrington's agents closed in, Bullitt begged Stidger to warn Dodd and Bowles. Both were arrested but Stidger was secretly released after "questioning" by government agents. Stidger raced toward Indiana, reporting his route to Carrington. Word had spread quickly. "Dodd was so excited at Bullitt's arrest that he grated his teeth, pulled at his hair and walked the floor many times," Stidger wrote. "There was no living man that could obtain the information in detail as he was now going to give it to me …. That he would even now go ahead and attempt to carry out the designs of the order." Greek fire was to be used to set Louisville on fire while armed members of the order would "rush into the city and take possession."

And Stidger wrote, "Dodd gave me this information … leaving the heads of the order in Louisville to carry out the details with my advice and assistance." Dodd's Grand Secretary Harrison, Lambdin Milligan and General Andrew Humphreys were summoned. "William A. Bowles was fully advised, and prepared to carry out any orders given."[67]

Arrests and weapons seizures followed upon Stidger's final report. Carrington quickly informed Ohio authorities: "Have seized 400 revolvers, 135,000 rounds of ammunition … and Grand Seal of Sons of Liberty with rituals and correspondence in office of H. H. Dodd, Grand Commander for the state."

A document that came to be known as the Carrington Report was published. On August 1, the Indianapolis *Daily Gazette*'s editorial praised Carrington's evidence and underscored the danger to the Union posed by the Sons of Liberty: "It is shown that the members of this order place the rules and oaths of the Order above the obligations of the laws of the land … and propose to levy war on the government." And about the once "true" soldiers snared in the dragnet, the paper stated, "They are none the less traitors now…. Benedict Arnold was once a true soldier and citizen; but when he turned traitor and the evidence was made public, the fact of his former loyalty did not set it aside…."

The *Indianapolis Daily Journal* of July 30 echoed much the same sentiment and trumpeted the public disclosures with bold, dramatic headlines: "Treason in Indiana. Exposé of the Sons of Liberty. Treasonable Nature of the Order. It is Both Civil and Military. Northern and Southern Traitors Worked Together."

Dodd slipped through the dragnet and escaped to Minnesota, but not for long. Upon his return to Ohio in early September, the wily old commander was immediately arrested along with Stidger and other leaders. Stidger spent "some weeks in jail, shifted from prison to prison" as members of the Sons "sympathized" with him. Carrington's agents arranged Stidger's escape, and Bullit "was released on parole…. He fled to Canada where he remained for two years."[68]

The government would not make the same mistake with the others.

Shortly after filing his last dispatch on the morning of September 1, Stidger married Josephine McGill. Immediately they left Louisville for Mattoon, Illinois, to honeymoon, far from the rumblings of revolution and mayhem. It was not to last.

On the night of September 14, 1864, General Carrington sent an urgent wire imploring his all-important spy to come in not from the cold but from his honeymoon. With Carrington, in a room barely lit by tiny gas lamps over an Indianapolis theatre, was Lieutenant Colonel Henry L. Burnett, Judge Advocate of the Ohio and Northern departments. Burnett was there to try the leaders of the Sons of Liberty for conspiracy against the United States. If found guilty, Indianapolis Grand Commander Harrison H. Dodd, Indiana lawyer Lambdin P. Milligan, Deputy Grand Commander of the Indiana order Horace Heffren, Dr. William Bowles, and the less prominent Andrew Humphreys and Stephen Horsey faced death by hanging.

The government's ability to convict rested solely on Stidger's testimony. If he didn't answer Carrington's urgent summons, the trial could not proceed. If Stidger did agree to testify, he was as good as dead. Hours passed without an answer. The long night got longer.

Stidger had every reason to ignore the summons. He was wary, exhausted and in love. And on September 15, he received Carrington's telegram. Obviously he agonized, probably Josie McGill entreated him not to leave. But Stidger insisted that he had to see Carrington in person, immediately.

"I took my wife and went to Indianapolis that night," he wrote. After assuring Stidger that he would not be forced to testify, Carrington played on Stidger's uncommon patriotism. "General Carrington told me that he was satisfied from the work that I had done and the hazardous risks that I had taken, that I would not now permit these men to be released without trial ... it did not take me one minute to decide. While I knew the additional hazard of my life that I was taking, I had never yet withheld any assistance from our government ... and I should not do so in this case."[69]

Immediately, an order convening the Military Commission was delivered and the government set to work preparing the charges and specifications. These were ready for the opening session in the U.S. courtrooms in Indianapolis on September 22. The first to be arraigned was Harrison H. Dodd, "a citizen of the state of Indiana, United States of America."[70]

Engraving of the accused Northwest conspirators "arraigned at Indianapolis for Treason." Frontispiece of the official transcript of *The Trials for Treason at Indianapolis, 1865.*

Before the trial began, Stidger was isolated far out of sight. Dodd, he reported earlier, was almost jovial, "having the same self confident air … appearing and speaking pleasantly to all."[71]

A military commission, Dodd's defense stated, could not possibly try him legally, and his counsel entered into a lengthy protest. They argued that he was not in uniform, civilian courts were open and functioning in Indianapolis, and he was a respected city elder. Judge Advocate Henry L. Burnett immediately objected, citing Lincoln's earlier proclamation ordering all who aided and abetted the enemy be put under martial law. The entire commission, Brigadier General Silas Cosgrove, Colonel William E. McLean, Colonel John T. Wilder, Colonel Thomas I. Lucas, Colonel Charles D. Murray, Colonel Benjamin Spooner and Colonel Richard P. DeHart unanimously overruled the aging physician's objections. His arraignment was ordered to proceed on Tuesday, September 22.

The charges were clear. The punishment: death by hanging.

> Conspiracy against the government of the United States: In this, that the said Harrison H. Dodd did with William A. Bowles of Indiana, Joshua F. Bullitt of Kentucky, Richard Barrett of the State of Missouri and others, did conspire against the government and duly constituted authorities of the United States, and did join himself to and secretly organize and disseminate, a secret society … known as the Sons of Liberty, having a civil and military organization … for the purpose of overthrowing the government and duly constituted authorities of the United States.

The charges continued, a catalogue of treason. All were punishable by death.

> Affording aid and comfort to rebels against the authority of the United States … said Dodd, then and there … did design and plot to communicate with the enemies of the United States … that should, in large force, invade the territory of the United States, to-wit the States of Kentucky, Indiana and Illinois.…[72]

Stidger related that "When he [Dodd] was brought into the courtroom [and] had the same self-confident air and expression of countenance," it was not to last.

The charges continued still yet:

> Inciting insurrection … said Harrison H. Dodd did, during a time of war between the United States and armed enemies of the United States,

organize and attempt to arm a portion of the citizens of the United States ... with the intent to induce them ... to throw off the authority of the United States and cooperate with an armed insurrection....[73]

The charges of "disloyal practices" and "violation of the laws of war" ended the prosecution's litany. The accused pleaded "not guilty." Immediately and without ceremony, the government's star witness was summoned: "At the calling of my name by the Judge Advocate, Dodd turned a deathly pale, or white," Stidger wrote. "As I approached the witness chair he stared at me in bewildered surprise, as though he found it difficult to believe his own sense of sight and hearing."[74]

Stidger was on the witness stand for two full days. Aside from corroborating his own reports to the government, Stidger revealed for the first time the secret codes, greetings, stances and passwords used by members of the Sons of Liberty. Because the rituals were passed verbally and never written down, Stidger's knowledge was invaluable. Exhausting in recitation, perhaps, but invaluable:

> If you are a member of the vestibule degree, and you meet a stranger ... you test him ... thus: You place the heel of your right foot in the hollow of the left, with the right hand under the left arm, bringing the left hand under the right arm, thus folding the arms and placing the four fingers of the left hand over the right arm. The stranger ... if a member of the order will take the same position.[75]

And that was just the beginning of the covert communications. Trust did not come easily. The rest continued in private. "You advance your right foot, and he will advance his right foot to meet yours. The two then take an ordinary grip with the right hands, at the same time placing the right hand on the right breast. If you find him incorrect, you stop."[76]

A verbal exchange of passwords followed with each party interjecting the correct letters: "the word Calhoun spelled backward, Nu-Oh-Lac -S-L — Give me liberty or give me death." A shake of the hand, if necessary was a "signal of distress ... placing the hand on the right breast, and raising the right hand and arm to their full height once, if it is in daytime. If at night ... you give the word Oak-un three times ... Oak is the tree of the acorn, which is the symbolical emblem of the order, and 'oun' is the last syllable of the password as it is usually pronounced."[77]

As the initiate climbed by degrees, the foot and hand signals became more complex, with new verbal exchanges: "If you go to the East-I will go to the West. Let there be no strife between mine and thine, for we be brethren-O-S-L — Resistance to tyrants — is obedience to God."[78]

Higher degrees demanded further signs, one representing the Southern Cross and, of course, more interactive chants: "Whence — Seir — How by the ford. Name it-Jayback. Thy password — Washington-Bayard ... Washington is the password of the degree." And finally, Stidger testified, admission was granted to the council's gatherings. "If you are known, you are admitted. If not, a committee is sent out to examine you ... they test you, and if they find you perfect in every particular, they admit you. If you fail in any respect, they know you no more."[79]

A stoic Felix Stidger endured lengthy cross-examinations, including questions of his own loyalty. The trial transcript dutifully recorded by Benn Pitman and printed in 1865 is in the possession of the present author. So clear were the connections, so direct the testimony (many lesser Sons named in the Stidger testimony turned state's evidence), and the parade of witnesses that followed confirmed and detailed Stidger's assertions. "The New York arms merchant described his sale of revolvers and ammunition, its shipment of Sunday school books.... An Illinois Copperhead told the story of the Sons of Liberty in that state, its military troops and plans for revolt. An Indiana informer gave similar testimony, and included the plan to attempt to seize Governor Morton, and to kill him should he resist,"[80] historian G.F. Milton wrote.

But on October 7, the day the court reconvened, a major setback: 'Prisoner" Dodd had escaped.

The government had foolishly promised the old seditionist he would not rot in a prison cell during his trial when on his "word of honor" he vowed not to escape. Harrison H. Dodd, accused of "capital and infamous crimes," was confined to the third floor of a room at the Indianapolis post office building. On Friday morning, October 7, 1864, he shimmied down a large rope provided by a friend in the street below and vanished. Remarkably, his abettors guided him to safety in Canada. There is no record of a large, armed pursuit.

The *Indianapolis Journal* of October 8 issued Carrington's indignant response: "The exposure of the Sons of Liberty has been made, every word is true. Harrison H. Dodd, Grand Commander of Indiana, has been on trial. Proof was overwhelming. Night before last he escaped from the third story window by a rope. Innocent men do not do so. The act confesses the guilt...."

The trial temporarily adjourned. Upon resumption, and after further deliberation, the military commission found Dodd guilty of all charges and sentenced him to be hanged. Judge Advocate Holt and the commanding general of the commission approved Dodd's sentence.

When the trial resumed on October 21, the same charges were leveled against Bowles, Humphreys, Heffren, Milligan and Horsey. Stidger, the principal witness, was again called to the stand. Facing in all probability the same dark fate, Heffren turned state's witness, providing "conclusive data both on the scheme of the organization and on the later plot for revolution," Milton wrote. The trial continued until December 1, with an array of "Indiana small fry," as Milton termed them, adding to the body of evidence against the Sons of Liberty.

The verdicts came fast and hard — guilty as charged. Bowles, Milligan and Horsey were sentenced to hang without having been able to utter a single word in their own defense. "The order for the carrying out of the sentence fixed the date of execution to be Friday, May 19, 1865," Stidger wrote, adding a final ironic fact: "The gallows to carry out the sentence of the three to be hanged was built in Indianapolis by rebel prisoners taken from Camp Morton." Andrew Humphreys "was sentenced to imprisonment for life," Stidger noted. The sentence was ultimately changed to "confinement within the boundaries of two townships in his own county."[81]

"By the time the military commission rendered its decision," Chief Justice William H. Rehnquist said in remarks given at the Indiana School of Law on October 28, 1996, "Lincoln had won re-election by a substantial margin."[82] Moreover, Atlanta was in Union hands and Sherman's march to the sea had broken the back of the Confederacy. Rehnquist believed that the executions might be met with disgust by a public grown weary of the agonies of war and tales of wicked Copperheads lurking in the darkness. Pleas of the lawyers for the condemned did not go unanswered. And President Lincoln, "who had to approve all death sentences imposed by military courts,"[83] was petitioned.

Without promising commutation of the sentences, Lincoln implied he might in time set the convictions aside, unaware that he had a scant few weeks to live. In the tumble of events, the assassination and the subsequent climate of rage and mourning, President Andrew Johnson ordered the executions to go ahead after pushing forward the date of the hangings to June 2, 1865. On May 30, at exactly "9:30 o'clock," according to

Stidger, President Andrew Johnson commuted the sentences of Bowles and Milligan to "imprisonment for life in the penitentiary at Columbus, Ohio."[84]

Immediately, Lambdin Milligan's attorney challenged the convictions, citing the Habeas Corpus Act of 1863. A petition was presented to the Circuit Court of the United States for the District of Indiana citing Milligan's unlawful imprisonment and demanding his release. When the Circuit Court divided over whether civilian courts had jurisdiction, "Under the procedures which then prevailed," Rehnquist wrote, "the case went to the Supreme Court under the name of *ex parte* Milligan."[85]

For six days in the beginning of March 1866, lawyers for the defendant and the government argued the case. Of enormous import was the challenge of the post–Civil War courts to reverse the suspension of civil liberties ordered and executed by the Lincoln administration. At issue was the need for a working democracy to reinstate the liberties won by founding Americans, no matter what the internal climate of the country. Of the nine Justices, President Lincoln had appointed five. Would the Justices, many in the country wondered, remember the uncommonly humane Lincoln's admonition, "With malice toward none, with charity for all"?

"At the close of the term in April," Rehnquist said, "the Court entered an order that the writ of habeas corpus sought by Milligan and the others should be granted, but that opinions in the case would not be filed until the beginning of the next term in December 1866. And while there was dissent, eventually all of the Justices "joined in rejecting the government's argument that the Bill of Rights simply did not apply in war time." However, the dissenting arguments were notable in that the Justices believed that "Congress, had it chosen to do so, could have authorized trials of certain civilians by military commission in a state such as Indiana, which had been invaded by Confederate forces and subjected to a widespread conspiracy."[86]

In 1866, as the South rejoiced at the verdicts that granted instant freedom to enemies of the state, the cell leaders melted easily back into lives of ease and privilege while Felix Stidger was a marked man.

But in spite of the best efforts of Stidger and others, plans to destroy a major American city were set in motion. A group of young Confederate soldiers sent to Canada and funded by the Confederate government were primed and ready to strike.

FOUR

Fire in the Night

"Suppose the plot had succeeded...would the sight of the charred bodies of thousands of our best citizens, their wives and their innocent children, have provoked a smile?"
New York Leader, November 1865

"I concluded to go and see how my fires were doing."
Lieutenant John William Headley, CSA*

He might have been mistaken for an errant schoolboy, or, perhaps, in his sumptuous surroundings, a young urban dandy. He was neither. On the evening of November 25, 1864, as part of an orchestrated act of terror aimed at the people of New York City, Confederate Lieutenant John William Headley poured Greek fire over room 204 of the elegant Astor House Hotel on lower Broadway.

Block-by-block, hotel-by-hotel, mission leader Lieutenant Colonel Robert Maxwell Martin, Captain Robert Cobb Kennedy, a hair-trigger Louisiana native who had been expelled from West Point, lieutenants John T. Ashbrook, James T. Harrington and James Chenault of Kentucky, John Price of Maryland, and one unknown man were doing the same.

They were a ready band, escapees from Johnson's Island prison camp, men who had ridden with the legendary Confederate raider John Hunt Morgan. Some were in stolen Yankee garb, others sported new top hats and fine suits on their backs, their pockets bulging with Confederate funds (the cell had been sent out of Canada), and for a short while were living easy and eating well in the city they were ordered to destroy.

Before the night was over, 19 major hotels throughout Manhattan's

*John W. Headley, Confederate Operations in Canada and New York *(New York and Washington: The Neale Publishing Company, 1906), p. 275.*

business district had been fired. A boisterous mix of old and new buildings, the entire city was a potential tinderbox. On his first visit to New York in 1854, Englishman Charles Cooper repeatedly described hearing the ominous clang of fire alarms day after day. With interest and awe, he surveyed the hubbub and bustle of the city, "looking eastward from Trinity Tower ... amid the closely packed banks and mercantile houses, the Treasury Building and Custom House." The streets of lower Manhattan were "crowded by ... carts, omnibuses ... as art all times to render it difficult sometimes impossible to cross...."[1]

Lieutenant Colonel Robert M. Martin, CSA, commander of the New York City arson cell (from *Confederate Operations in Canada and New York* by John William Headley, collection of the New-York Historical Society).

Packed cheek to jowl were hotels and government buildings — the centers of tourism, intrigue and commerce made of stone, wood or glistening marble, some boasting private bathrooms and moving stairs. And close to the glitter and glamour were hundreds of wooden tenements, teeming "rookeries" imperiled by rotten, aging wood. With a volunteer fire force and "engine houses [that] became loitering places for the idle and the young," the quelling of fires was erratic at best. It was upon inside knowledge of the unreliable system that the Confederate cell relied.[2]

John William Headley recounted plans for the attack long after the war when punishment was no longer possible. His book *Confederate Operations in Canada and New York,* a remarkable volume peppered with self-justification and large dollops of pride and zealotry, details the plot to destroy New York City: "The presidential election which was to be held on the 8th day of November ... and was deemed an opportune time for the blow to be struck at Chicago and in New York. Colonel [Jacob]

Thompson advised us that detachments under Captain Churchill in Cincinnati and Dr. Luke Blackburn in Boston would set fires to those cities on Election Day."[3]

The plans for whole-scale mayhem that had so worried Felix Stidger and the United States authorities were not unexpected. And there was a warning, interpreted by historians as a clear signal for the plot to go forward, not as one might guess in the form of a whispered confidence or a coded dispatch, but in a brazen newspaper editorial that appeared in the *Richmond Whig* on October 15, 1864. *The New York Times* reprinted it in full on October 19:

> Sheridan reports to Grant that, in moving down the Valley to Woodstock, he has burned over two thousand barns filled with wheat, hay and farming implements, over seventy mills filled with flour and wheat. This was done by order of Grant himself, commander of all the Yankee armies. It is only the execution in part of the order to destroy everything in the Valley that will sustain life. The fell work is still going on. Now, it is an idle waste of words to denounce this sort of war. We simply have to regard it as a practical matter, and ask ourselves how it is to be met. There is one effectual way, and only one that we know of, to arrest and prevent this and every other sort of atrocity — and that is to burn one of the chief cities of the enemy, say Boston, Philadelphia or Cincinnati, and let its fate hang over the others as a warning of what might be done to them, if the present system of war on the part of the enemy is continued. If we are asked how such a thing can be done — we answer, nothing would be easier. A million dollars would lay the proudest city of the enemy in ashes. The men to execute the work are already there. There would be no difficulty in finding there, here or in Canada, suitable persons to take charge of the enterprise and arrange its details. Twenty men with plans all preconcerted, and means provided, selecting some dry, windy night, might fire Boston in a hundred places and wrap it up in flames from center to suburb. They might retaliate on Richmond, Charleston, &c? [In original.] Let them do so if they dare. It is a game at which we can beat them. New York is worth twenty Richmonds. They have a dozen or so towns to our one, and in their towns is centered all their wealth. It would be immoral and barbarous? It is not immoral and barbarous to defend yourself by any means, or with any weapon the enemy may employ for your destruction. They chose to substitute the torch for the sword. We may so use their weapon as to make them repent, literally in sackcloth and ashes, that they ever adopted it....

It was not unusual to see such direct and inflammatory journalistic opinions expressed during the war. Coded messages, even details of troop movements, were carried by both sides. According to author Nat Brandt, "Cryptic advertisements were run in certain Northern newspapers that were available in Richmond. Confederate officials there, in turn, ran personals in the Richmond papers with the addendum, 'New York papers, please copy!'" And, often, Copperhead papers like the *New York Daily News* ran the ads. With such bold and explicit cries for vengeance encouraged, or as some historians believe, planted by the Confederate apparatus in Canada, the plan went forward.

As Stidger and others had warned, the upcoming conflagrations were intended as diversionary tactics so that armed Copperheads could take over government buildings, free prisoners from Fort Lafayette, prevent the re-election of President Lincoln, and raise the Confederate flag over the city.

Headley acted on orders from Jacob Thompson. He later wrote, "It was arranged that we should arrive in New York about ten days before the election and become familiar with the streets and localities of the city." Headley and his party of eight left Toronto traveling in pairs, "though we all went on the same train by the New York Central Railroad from the Suspension Bridge."[4]

With letters of introduction to the group's handlers from Jacob Thompson and plenty of ready money, the men registered at separate New York City hotels under assumed names and went directly to the office of their chief handler, James A. McMaster, the editor of the Copperhead-friendly *Freeman's Journal* and an acknowledged secessionist sympathizer, described by Headley as a man "of large proportions ... at least 6 feet 3 inches, without much flesh...."[5]

"Mr. McMasters [*sic*] was the practical head of the operations in New York," Headley wrote. "We assured him he could rely on us for open, bold and unflinching action when the hour arrived for crucial duty." In fact, McMaster, along with Captain Longmire (actually the music professor and scholar Emile Longuemare) of Missouri as well as agents of Governor Seymour assured Headley's men that all was at the ready.

A supply of Greek fire was being brought from Canada to New York and would be ready for pick-up in short order. "The city authorities were our friends ... McMasters [*sic*] told us he would request Governor Seymour to send a confidential agent down to the city with whom he wished us to confer," Headley reported. And, he added, "Indeed, we were to have the support of the Governor's official neutrality."[6]

The "official neutrality" of select New York leaders was well known to the Confederates in Canada. It was by careful design and assurances of support at the highest levels that Headley's cell was ordered on the mission. In spite of its location, far from the arenas of war to the South, New York was a city ravaged by dissonance and governed by anti–Lincoln Southern sympathizers.

In 1857 Fernando Wood was reelected mayor of New York City with the assistance of the infamous Dead Rabbits gang who brazenly stuffed the ballot boxes with votes of people long deceased. Wood was secretly a member of the anti-immigrant Know Nothing Party and outwardly a champion of the disenfranchised Irish and German immigrant population. The well-known duplicitous nature of the wealthy, roguish tobacco merchant kept both enemies and friends in a constant state of flux.

In 1861, when the war began, Wood proposed that New York City secede from the state as well as the Union and become a free and independent city. He never failed to express a common sympathy with residents of the Confederacy.

To further promote this common sympathy, Wood purchased the *New York Daily News*, installing his trusted brother Benjamin as its editor. The Wood brothers, pro–Southern, pro-slavery sympathizers, had an uncensored forum throughout most of the war.

Benjamin Wood refused to fly the American flag over the *Daily News* office building and refused to quiet the paper's strident anti–Lincoln rhetoric. He faced an outraged grand jury and was accused of giving aid and comfort to the enemy. Avoiding formal charges that would show the world just how polarized the great city was, the Postmaster General forbid the paper the use of U.S. mail for delivery. Defiant and unrepentant, Wood hired the railroads to do it. Formally stung, the government ordered Wood to cease publication for eighteen months, but their act did not quell the ardor of the paper's faithful.

In 1863, Wood was back in business using the paper to publish classifieds with encoded messages from Richmond and the Davis government itself—formally, if not tacitly, an act of treason. He was not alone. Many Copperheads were emboldened by the bloody Draft Riots, repeatedly inflaming sensibilities by using newspaper editorials to incite the already outraged sentiments of many New Yorkers.

When summarizing the Confederate plots out of Canada, Jacob Thompson, the acting head of Confederate Canadian operations, told

Confederate Secretary of State Judah Benjamin, "Besides a crowd of less distinguished persons, I saw during the course of the summer [1864], in some instances repeatedly, Governor Seymour of New York ... and Benjamin Wood...."[7]

New York Governor Horatio Seymour, also a well known Lincoln hater, assured Jacob Thompson and the leaders of the Sons of Liberty that in the event of an uprising in New York he would remain "neutral," a code for inaction should perpetrators of insurrection take to the streets.

John Headley understood "that the governor would not use the militia to suppress the insurrection in the city but would leave the duty to the authorities in Washington." Further assured by the governor's private secretary that "we could prosecute our plans accordingly," Headley and his men proceeded to the piano store of Jacob Thompson's operative, Confederate agent W. Larry McDonald, where their trunks were secreted and further instructions were given. While awaiting final orders from McMaster, the men went out on the town and proceeded to enjoy "a period of enjoyment and recreation in most respects."[8]

Like eager tourists sightseeing, the men went to the theatre, heard a sermon by Henry Ward Beecher, attended a lecture given by Artemis Ward, and watched Lincoln's presidential opponent Union General George B. McClellan "review a monster torchlight procession" from the balcony of the Fifth Avenue Hotel. Headley and his band stood in the throngs filling Madison Square, heartened by the anti–Lincoln sentiments they heard along the way. "The President was caricatured in many ludicrous and ungainly pictures ... the spirit of revolt was manifest," Headley crowed, "and it only needed a start and a new leadership."[9]

They waited for the final go-ahead from their hideout, a cottage on the edge of Central Park secured for them by Longuemare. The orders to proceed did not come. Worse, forewarned of an impending insurrection, 10,000 soldiers under the command of the feared Union General Benjamin Butler, known as "the Beast" to his enemies, arrived in the city. Relief and praise abounded at the news of Butler's arrival.

The *New York Times* of November 5 gloated at the news of Butler's arrival: "The wisdom of the government in selecting a man who had scattered the howling rabble of New Orleans like chaff ... approved itself to the conscience of every patriot and made Copperheads squirm and writhe in torture. Malcontents, if there be, dare not resort to extremes ... a strong military force is already disposed to nip all disorders in the bud."

The editorial went on to acknowledge dire warnings of "villainous threats made by Richmond papers of laying New York, Buffalo, and other Northern cities in ashes...."

Demoralized by the reports, but unfailingly committed to the mission at hand, John Headley believed the upcoming terrorist act was completely justified. In bold block letters recorded for all of posterity he wrote,

> It is fair to all concerned to record the fact here: TEN DAYS BEFORE THIS ATTEMPT OF CONFEDERATES TO BURN NEW YORK CITY, GENERAL SHERMAN HAD BURNED THE CITY OF ATLANTA, GEORGIA, AND THE NORTHERN PAPERS AND PEOPLE OF THE WAR PARTY WERE IN GREAT GLEE OVER THE MISERIES OF THE SOUTHERN PEOPLE.[10]

Lieutenant John William Headley, CSA, 1865. Headley was second in command of the arson terror cell that attemted to burn New York City on November 25, 1864 (from *Confederate Operations in Canada and New York* by John William Headley, collection of The New-York Historical Society).

Justifications aside, Headley's handlers were losing heart. After hearing the news of impending Union troop arrivals, McMaster summoned the band, "fearing," Headley said, "our plans could not be carried to consummation." Disheartened by Lincoln's reelection and the absence of uprisings in Chicago and Boston and by now afraid for his own skin should the men act on their own, McMaster told the band that a conference of leaders decided that action was to be postponed. "The more we insisted on the attempt in New York the weaker McMasters [*sic*] became," Headley admitted, remembering that the men had promised Jacob Thompson the destruction of New York, no matter what happened in other cities. Pressed by Martin and Headley, Captain Longuemare reluctantly gave the name and address of the chemist who had made the Greek fire, and fled to upstate New York, "until the sensation was over" or the men lost heart and faded away.[11]

The men did nothing of the sort. Instead, they lobbied for the attack to be launched on Thanksgiving Day. To a man, all their contacts backed out, stating, "Their connection with the proposed attack was foredoomed to failure."[12]

There was to be no such failure. Defiantly, Martin assigned Headley the perilous task of picking up the Greek fire and added that the chemicals had been paid for in advance. Following McMaster's directions, threading his way through the narrow byways of Greenwich Village, Headley found the chemist, an old man in a dark basement shop "on the west side of Washington Place, off Washington Square."[13]

He was "wearing a long beard all over his face," Headley wrote.

After telling the chemist he was there to pick up Longuemare's "valise," the old man wordlessly handed him a "two and a half foot long" suitcase so heavy Headley "had to change hands every ten steps to carry it."[14] Unable to find a carriage, Headley lugged the chemical-laden carrier to City Hall Square and boarded a streetcar for the Central Park safe house. Once inside the packed interior of the car, Headley noticed a heavy odor of sulfur, "a little like rotten eggs." Other passengers began to complain; "There must be something dead in that valise," one of them reportedly said as Headley hefted the suitcase off the car.[15]

Safe in the cottage hideout, Headley opened the valise to find that a bottle of the incendiary, "a liquid resembling water," had indeed broken, its stench filling the room. The chemical weapon, relied upon to torch a city, was as yet an unknown commodity. "None of the party knew anything about Greek fire," Headley admitted, "except that the moment it was exposed to air it would blaze and burn everything it touched."[16]

With the mission set to begin promptly at eight o'clock the following evening, the men parted, hurrying to rent the hotel rooms they had already cased. When two cell members did not return to the house by six the following evening, Headley, Martin, Chenault, Ashbrook, Kennedy and Harrington agreed to launch the attack as planned. They poured the liquid into well-sealed bottles, and packed 12 dozen into the valise.

"It had been agreed that our fires would be started at the hotels, so as to do the greatest damage in the business district on Broadway,"

Headley stated. With ten bottles of Greek fire each, some in satchels, others wrapped in paper and stuffed into overcoats purchased for the occasion, "We were now ready to create a sensation in New York." And the city Headley hoped to destroy was alive with celebration, its residents blissfully unaware of the burning and destruction that was to take place that night.[17]

November 25 was a holiday, ironically called Evacuation Day, "commemorating the eighty-first anniversary of the day in 1773 when the last British troops left New York City." A cold wind and pelting rain that might have kept crowds off the streets had stopped and the evening was cold and clear.[18]

Rob Kennedy fired his room at the New England Hotel, and then proceeded to Lovejoys on Park Row opposite City Hall Park to do the same. James Chenault poured Greek fire on the floor of room 44 of the Howard on lower Broadway, and Ashbrook and Harrington torched room 139 of the St. Nicholas, a white marble 600-room wonder at Prince and Broadway. Later Ashbrook set his room at the LaFarge House on fire, but not before he asked a servant girl for matches. "Passing the room a moment later, the girl concluded that he'd forgotten to turn off the gas ... a bright light in the transom lit up the hall like a bolt of lightning."[19]

Next to the LaFarge House, in their one and only appearance together, the famous Booth brothers, Junius, Edmond and John, were performing *Julius Caesar* to a standing room only crowd, the slight smell of smoke from the LaFarge House not yet a cause for panic.

The mission commander, Robert Martin, took care of room 148 of the Fifth Avenue Hotel, a favored haunt of Southern travelers and precious metal dealers, room 84 at the St. James, and the Belmont on Fulton Street. At the Astor, after heaping chairs, bureau drawers, newspapers and bedding in the middle of the room, Headley slowly opened a vial of Greek fire and poured it over the pile. Remembering to lock the door behind him, he walked quickly down the hall of the six story, three hundred-room hotel and out into the street. Within minutes the room was in flames.

Nearby, at the City Hotel, Headley did the same, pouring the Greek fire and racing out the door, pausing only to glance across the street to see that a bright light flared in a window of the Astor.

Headley next demanded a room at the United States Hotel, "signed the roster as 'William B. Brown' and was given room 172 on the fifth floor."[20]

Again, Headley made quick use of the liquid fire, but when he noticed the clerk regarding him suspiciously, he quickly melted into the night. Fire alarms began to sound. "As I came back to Broadway it seemed that a hundred bells were ringing," Headley said. "I concluded to go and see how my fires were doing."[21]

Fire brigades tore through the streets, manned by strapping Irishmen who insisted on pulling the engines themselves rather than riding behind the dray horses bred for the job. Flames poured from the windows of the posh LaFarge House on Broadway. A smoke-filled hallway sent a chambermaid crawling out the window of the Metropolitan Hotel on Prince Street.

A seven foot tall giantess plunged through the panicked crowd at the Barnum Museum and ran wailing into the street. "A great crowd was pouring out of Barnum's Museum, nearly opposite the Astor," Headley reported, thrilled to see people struggling to escape the building, getting down ladders, crawling out of third floor windows, and witnessing "the manager crying for help to get his animals out."[22]

This, according to Headley was good news. Phineas T. Barnum's American Museum, which housed a jumble of animals, freaks and frauds, was not on the target list. Thinking it would be "fun to start a scare," Robert Kennedy later told Headley that he hurled a bottle of Greek fire against a stairwell of the museum. "It looked like people were getting hurt running over each other in the stampede," Headley wrote, adding that most people feared there had been an attack by the Confederates.[23]

At the Winter Garden Theatre, Edwin Booth stopped dead in the middle of the performance of *Julius Caesar* and begged a sold out crowd to stay calm. At the climactic end of a performance of *The Corsican Brothers* at Niblo's Garden, cheers mixed with cries of horror as "someone in the gallery shouted, 'Fire!' Up in the balcony, men tried to hold back others from throwing themselves down to the parquet."[24]

Excited by what he had seen, Headley walked down Broadway toward the North River Wharf and according to plan, "jerked a bottle in six different places ... aiming for vessels and barges of every description ... they were ablaze before I left ... there were wild scenes here the last time I looked back."[25]

As the alarms screamed and people poured into the streets, Headley headed for a pre-arranged rendezvous with his cohorts on Bowery Street across from the Metropolitan Hotel. As he walked, he saw Rob Kennedy up ahead: "I closed up behind him and slapped him on the shoulder."

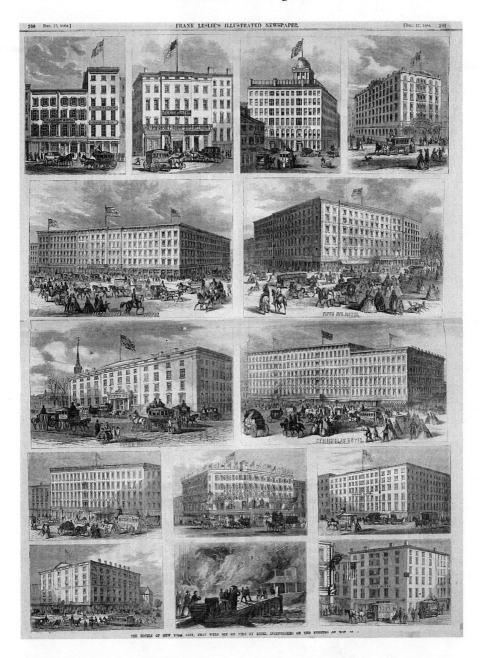

"Hotels in lower Manhattan that were set on fire by rebel incendiaries" (from *Frank Leslie's Illustrated Newspaper*, December 17, 1864, collection of the New-York Historical Society).

Kennedy wheeled around, gun drawn. "I laughed and he knew me ... and said he ought to shoot me for giving him such a scare." Eagerly, the men compared notes. Not only had Kennedy fired all the hotels on his list, a new, unplanned target opportunity arose. "He concluded to go down to Barnum's Museum ... coming down the stairway it occurred to him that there it would be fun to start a scare." Kennedy broke a bottle of Greek fire "on the edge of the step like he would crack an egg. It blazed up and he got out to witness the result."[26]

Later, Asbrook and Harrington told Headley and Kennedy they had witnessed "the wildest excitement imaginable" and had heard "the opinion expressed generally that the rebels were in the city to destroy it."[27]

Headley and his band slipped away into the tumultuous night, joking, backslapping, and laughing again about how some of the bottles had cracked like eggs. But amid the levity, there was a growing realization: Greek fire had failed to destroy New York City. After "observing that the fires had been put out in all the places as easily as any ordinary fire," Headley remembered, "we came to the conclusion that Longmire [*sic*] and his ... chemist had put up a job on us after it was found that we could not be dissuaded from our purpose."[28]

"Rare view of Broadway and City Hall Park looking north from the Astor House to Chambers Street..." (collection of the New-York Historical Society).

It was possible. The solution may have been watered down. But more probably the arsonists did not realize that the incendiary needed oxygen to fully combust. In their caution to avoid detection, most if not all of the men reportedly closed the doors of their rooms and probably did not think to open windows and raise drapes, thus preventing the Greek fire from consuming the hotels. Or, as Headley later suspected, the men had been betrayed.

After separating from the band, Headley and Martin checked into a hotel at two A.M. and went to sleep. The next morning, after they had rested well while the city endured a night of sheer terror, they went to a restaurant "on Broadway near Twelfth" for a leisurely breakfast, bought the morning papers and were surprised to see "the entire front pages were given up to sensational accounts...." Splashed in bold type, ringing with alarm and disbelief, the *New York Times* revealed what was so far known of the plots and plotters:

> THE REBEL PLOT. ATTEMPT TO BURN THE CITY. ALL THE PRINCIPAL HOTELS SET ON FIRE. THE FIRES PROMPTLY EXTINGUISHED. PROMPT ARREST OF REBEL EMMISSARIES. THE POLICE ON THE TRACK OF OTHERS.

The brief story written in the dead of night when many details were still unknown, continued:

> The city was startled last evening by the loud and simultaneous clanging of fire-bells in every direction ... a pre-concerted attempt was being made by rebel emissaries, in accordance with the fiendish program recently set forth by the Richmond papers, to burn New York and other Northern Cities.... The scenes at the various hotels, where the usual quiet of the evening was broken by the alarm of fire, and by startling rumors of extensive conflagrations throughout the city.... The police are said to be on the track of several suspected persons.[29]

According to historian Nat Brandt, "All the newspapers in the city, pro–Lincoln and Copperhead alike, reacted to the plot with shock."[30]

Freeman's Journal editor James A. McMaster, aware of the identity of the entire cell, feigned surprise at the attack, but stopped short of accusing the Confederate leaders. "Can it be dreamed that the Confederate Government wanted to burn up the wives and children of these opponents of war?"[31] McMaster asked.

The *New York Herald* voiced confidence that "The wretches who would have destroyed all our principal hotels but one by fire, and caused the death of their harmless occupants, deserve no pity, and should they be detected ... should be hung up in as brief a space as possible and as soon as the law will permit."[32] Major General John A. Dix, headquartered in the city, concurred: "The attempt to set fire to New York is one of the great atrocities of the age.... There is nothing in the annals of barbarism which evinces greater vindictiveness. It was not a mere attempt to destroy the city but an effort to secure the greatest possible destruction of human life."[33]

General Dix promptly reissued an order to round up all Southerners living in the city who had long been assumed to be Confederate sympathizers. "Immediately, they must register with the army," Dix insisted. "If they are detected and proven as spies, they will be brought before a military commission and will be executed without the delay of a single day."[34]

Fire marshal Alfred E. Baker analyzed two of the Greek fire bottles left behind at the Fifth Avenue Hotel. "The preparation," he announced, "was found to be phosphorous dissolved in sulphuret of carbon. I had some of the mixture prepared, and found that by dissolving two parts of phosphorous into four parts of sulphuret of carbon the exact results were obtained. I found that a blaze was produced in from four to eight minutes."[35] According to Nat Brandt, "Baker believed that the plot failed not from any want of courage on the part of the conspirators, but from miscalculations as to the use of the combustible materials employed."

With ears to the ground and eyes on more newspapers, Headley and Martin learned "that the authorities had a full knowledge of the plot and the ring-leaders would be captured during the day." If the men were poised to flee, it was not apparent, even though Headley reported, "All our fictitious names registered at the different hotels were given and interviews with the clerks described us all." He added, "The clerk of the United States Hotel gave a minute description of my personal appearance, clothing, manners and actions." Perhaps the descriptions given by the witnesses might have applied to half the young clerks, soldiers and the dandies who roamed the city and prowled the hotels, saloons and brothels of the city.[36]

They were safe for the time, they thought. "As soon as we finished breakfast we slipped out and took a car on Bowery Street for central Park. Here we loafed, and read the afternoon papers," Headley related, "disappointed to learn the fires had not caused great damage."[37]

"The plan was excellently conceived … and had it been executed with one half the ability with which it was drawn up, no human power could have saved the city from utter destruction," The *New York Times* reported on November 27, adding that John Decker, chief of the fire department, had been forewarned, allowing some hotel security measures to be taken. Pails of water, not provided on a regular basis, were in fact placed in at least three of the hotels. Damages were assessed: "The St. Nicholas has probably suffered the worst … the damage there will probably amount to $3,000 dollars," the *Times* reported, a great deal of money during the Civil War. Other hotel damage estimates ranged from hundreds of dollars to a few thousand. Damage to the psyches of New Yorkers was incalculable.[38]

Convinced the authorities were on "a cold trail," Headley and Martin left Central Park and went to McDonald's piano store to pick up their luggage. McDonald's daughter Katie, "the moment she saw Colonel Martin shuddered, and putting her hand, palm outward … motioned him away."[39]

The men learned that the authorities knew more than they had been led to believe. In Headley's words: "The last issue of the Evening Post … stated that the plot of these rebels had been divulged to the authorities a month before by a man from Canada who had been promised one hundred thousand dollars for his information." Headley also claimed that detectives had been following the men around the city, but "they had finally abandoned us as a lot of well-behaved young men who simply seemed to be enjoying ourselves, and they never could trace us to any of the places where we would be supposed to go if we had any connection with the New York Sons of Liberty."[40] The informant in question provokes rousing discussion among modern historians.

Some believed, as did Headley, that Godfrey Joseph Hyams, a Confederate double agent operating in Canada, had betrayed the cell. Later, Hyams would reveal the plans to spread the deadly yellow fever engineered by Dr. Luke Pryor Blackburn throughout Northern cities. It is also possible that Felix Stidger's undercover work in the Sons of Liberty may have led authorities to shadow the New York arsonists.

The plot to burn New York *was* hatched in Canada over the summer of 1864 when spies, saboteurs, privateers and politicos swarmed through the Queen's Hotel in Toronto pitching their ideas for acts of terrorism to the representatives of President Jefferson Davis. A safe 400 miles from the din of battle, with Canadian cabals but distant rumors, many New Yorkers could not bring themselves to believe they had been imperiled.

As for the "well behaved young men who simply seemed to be enjoying [themselves]," the time to flee the city had arrived. "Colonel Martin and I decided ... that we had better meet our companions and arrange a plan to get out of New York and back to Canada," Headley wrote. When they reached the cottage safe house at six in the evening their cohorts also arrived. The men quickly scanned train schedules and learned that a New York Central train was leaving at 11 o'clock that night and that the sleepers would open for passengers at nine. At the depot, "two of the party who had boarded on a secluded street ventured to buy the tickets and succeeded" and once aboard the sleeper, "scrutinizing every passenger," to keep a close watch for detectives who might be casing the train, the men "examined the rear of our car and found a way to get out in case of a fight and a chase." The train pulled out of the city but the men remained vigilant until they "undressed for much-needed rest and sleep."[41]

Once in Albany, the ticketed destination, Headley and his band had to spend Sunday waiting for the late night train from Albany to Niagara and the suspension bridge to Canada. They scattered among the hotels in Albany, stayed hidden in their rooms and finally boarded the sleeper over the suspension bridge. "That night Colonel Martin and I gave a full account of our operations in New York to Colonel Jacob Thompson, upon whose orders the enterprise had been taken," Headley wrote.[42]

Later, in his report to Judah Benjamin, Thompson called the New York plot "a most daring attempt," blaming its failure on the choice of Greek fire as an incendiary: "Their reliance on the Greek fire has proved a misfortune. It cannot be depended upon as an agent in such work. I have no faith whatever in it, and no attempt shall hereafter be made, under my general directions with any such material."[43] In fact, Thompson would never again depend on Greek fire, but his government would. By February 1865, a new version of Greek fire was perfected and tested by Columbia University professor turned Confederate weapons maker Richard Sears McCulloh.

Deadly Greek fire was the last thing on the minds of Headley and his compatriots. After two days in Toronto, Katie McDonald arrived with bad news. New York police were closing in on the conspiracy and the conspirators, and detectives had gone to Toronto hoping to identify Headley's band based on information from General Dix. Immediately, Headley, Kennedy, Martin and Ashbrook went into hiding while detectives searched for clues.

According to Brandt, a sentry on patrol at the Johnson's Island Prison camp found an unsigned letter "stuffed into the outgoing letterbox ... addressed to the superintendent of the prison camp." The letter said: "Sir: It having come to my attention that one R.C. Kennedy ... who escaped this prison ... was in N. York at the time of the burning of some hotels." The letter went on to say that Kennedy, now in Toronto, had "admitted to being part of the plot to burn New York."[44]

Aside from exposing Rob Kennedy as one of the arsonists, further information reached Jacob Thompson regarding "seven Confederate generals who were to be removed from Johnson's Island in mid December for transfer by train to Fort Lafayette in New York Harbor .... Thompson, unwilling to admit defeat, hoped to waylay the train and free the officers."[45]

Astonishingly, Martin, Headley, Kennedy, Harrington, Ashbrook and five Confederate soldiers were ordered to Buffalo. The plan was "to capture the train carrying the Confederate generals, derail its coaches, and run the engine and Express Car closer to Buffalo before derailing them too."[46]

The men laid "a long iron rail from the road bed" across the tracks, but the train hurtled past them before the conductor halted the train. The men raced to the suspension bridge and headed back to Toronto in defeat. What might have been a last ditch effort for the Confederacy turned into a fiasco. What is notable about the failure is the utter willingness of the New York arsonists to risk life and limb once again and the near fanatical determination of Jacob Thompson to order the scheme. It was to be the last. Thompson was fast losing favor with Richmond and was soon to be replaced by a hardened military strategist, General Edwin Gray Lee. Now all Thompson could manage was to secure passports and money for the men.

And through a variety of ruses, detectives were closing in on the arsonists by posing as Southern sympathizers, gaining the confidence of Larry McDonald by damning Lincoln, and "spitting on the Union flag."[47] Convinced he was among friends, McDonald talked and gave a complete account of the plot and the six active arsonists, adding that they were headed home. Rob Kennedy was particularly anxious to rejoin his command, but it was to be his undoing. Thompson gave Kennedy a "Certificate of Citizenship," a document needed to "get through the Southern lines."[48] He left immediately with Ashbrook, traveling on the Grand Trunk Railway to Michigan. As the train stopped at the United States border and Kennedy slept, detectives boarded the car, walking the aisles and scanning the faces of the passengers. Having taken a separate seat, Ashbrook watched in horror as detectives grabbed Kennedy and yanked him from the train. "Kennedy submitted without a struggle,"[49] Headley reported. Ashbrook got away by escaping through a window into the darkness.

According to Headley, "Captain Kennedy was forwarded to New York City, where he was imprisoned in Fort Lafayette." Before his trial by military commission, Kennedy begged McMaster and editor Benjamin Wood to furnish him with $1500 for his freedom, a sum demanded by a Detective Edward Hays posing as a jailer. A fool's game, surely, as the men would rather see him dead than admit even a passing acquaintance.

Kennedy wrote the following letter on January 11, 1865:

> Hon. Benj. Wood Mulberry St. Prison
> Dear Sir
> I am a prisoner in the hands of my enemies, to be tried by court-martial as I am informed, for attempting to fire this city. I can be released for $1500 in gold as the bearer can inform you. Can you advance it for me? I could refund it as soon as I reach Canada as Hon. J. Thompson or my friend Mr. S.V. Mitchell I *know* would cheerfully furnish the means to do so. I live in Louisiana Claiborne Parish-not yet overrun by the Federals. If I could *only* see you, I am satisfied I could convince you of my ability to make it all right. Consider my life is at stake. Please answer per bearer verbally if you think best.
> Respectfully
> Your obt. Servt.
> Robert C. Kennedy
> Capt. C.S.A. 42[50]

And the hapless Kennedy incriminated himself repeatedly as he frantically sought to obtain the money. On January 18, he wrote to McMaster:

> Dear Sir-
> My Turnkey, the bearer of this, I have bribed to release me. If I can get some responsible man in the City to be my security — or can guarantee that the money will be forthcoming. He says if I can get such guarantee

for five hundred dollars he will get me out tonight. I have not time to explain matters or make suitable apologies for thus addressing you — an entire stranger .... Any arrangements you may make to effect my release will entitle you to my eternal gratitude. I can refund any sum under $1500 once I reach Canada. Burn this — stationary is dangerous....[51]

And three days later, Kennedy wrote another letter to McMaster, his growing desperation revealed in the increasingly familiar content of the letter.

The bearer Hays says he is not willing to effect my release unless he has other assurances than your mere word ... You know how I am situated — must risk treachery & foul play — but think there is no danger unless you commit yourself in writing ... if you can aid me without injuring yourself I ask you to do it — but if you have to place yourself in the hands of any son of a bitch ... Refuse altogether and leave me to my fate.

In a reckless postscript, Kennedy added: "You remember Stanton do you not?"[52] Of course, Stanton was Kennedy's false name when he registered in the hotels. Not lost on modern historians is the significance of the alias. Edwin M. Stanton was Lincoln's fierce and unforgiving Secretary of War.

Hays pressed Kennedy to admit his part in the fires, and Kennedy finally admitted he was indeed one of the New York arsonists. Immediately the government moved forward with a plan. Because he was behind Union lines in civilian clothes, it was determined that Robert Kennedy would be tried as a spy.

According to Nat Brandt, "a statement ... about his part in the fires and the names of the other conspirators would undoubtedly incline the court to leniency."[53] The "confession," recorded by a stenographer, was taken down immediately. It was a litany of omissions. Yes, Kennedy had been in New York.

I was in N.Y. city [sic] last Nov. at Belmont Hotel — came here from Toronto — on the hotel books as Mr. Stanton. I brought to Mr. Clarke [sic] a letter of introduction from Mr. W.L. McDonald. I came to spend a few weeks, have some fun & run the blockade to Wilmington. I had been confined at Johnson's I. [Island] & escaped. Was in N.Y. a few weeks. Left N.Y. in Nov. Did not leave N.Y. when I was at the Belmont....[54]

Kennedy went on and on, representing himself as a man on the town, in "citizen's dress," with not a word about the fires, and swore he was innocent. The government vowed to hang him at the first opportunity.

On January 31, Kennedy's trial began at the Department of the East's headquarters on Bleecker Street. Brigadier General Fitz-Henry Warren read the charges. There were six other officers present, and the charges were as follows:

Charge 1: Acting as a spy. "In this, that Robert C. Kennedy, a captain of the military service of the insurgent States, was found acting as a spy in the city of New York...."[55]

Charge 2: Violation of the laws of war. "In this, that Robert C. Kennedy ... undertook to carry on irregular and unlawful warfare in the city and State of New York by setting fire thereto...."[56]

Events happened rapidly. Kennedy pled not guilty. Detective Hays' testimony fully incriminated Kennedy, who had foolishly decided to defend himself. Witnesses followed with dizzying speed until Kennedy's former cell member John Price appeared for the prosecution. Price had not taken part in the actual hotel burnings and was trying desperately to save his own skin. Days turned into weeks as witnesses were summoned, none helping the accused. Kennedy, writing from "In Hell," as his diary entry was titled, awaited the verdict in his cell: "If I am executed, it will be nothing less than judicial, brutal, cowardly murder."[57]

Disappointed that Kennedy had not named his associates in the plot, the government transferred him to Fort Lafayette Prison in New York harbor to await the verdict. "The octagonal structure with thirty-foot walls and batteries commanding a view of the channel .... The open area within the fort was 120 feet across with a pavement 25 feet wide running around the inside, leaving a patch of ground 70 feet square in the center."[58]

Prisoners ranged from secessionist sympathizers to Union soldiers who had "turned coat" during the war to join the Confederacy. It was here that Robert Cobb Kennedy was to spend his final days: "Please inform Robert C. Kennedy ... that he has been condemned to death and the sentence has been approved. The time for his execution has not been fixed, but will probably not be later than the last of next week. He will have a previous notice of four or five days...."[59] The communication was signed by Major General John A. Dix.

Kennedy wrote a letter to his father soon after his conviction. "Dear Father: I have been condemned to die either as a spy or guerrilla, or perhaps as both....You know I am incapable of being either ... I have been guilty of no act that should cause you, mother or any of the children to blush for their son or brother. I am simply in the hands of my enemies and I am to die...."[60]

On March 14, Kennedy appealed to President Lincoln to review his case and grant clemency: "Please consider the character of the witnesses produced against me. It was not shown that I was ever in the City of New York after the 21st of Nov, four days previous to the occurrence of the fires for which I am condemned to die for kindling ... I throw myself entirely upon your clemency...."[61]

Before a response came, Dix ordered Kennedy's execution to go forward on Saturday, March 25, saying, "I desire him to understand that I have not said, and shall not say, anything to the president in opposition to such an exercise of mercy...."[62] Dix advised that Kennedy prepare for his execution. This author has not been able to determine whether or not Lincoln ever saw Kennedy's letter.

"I want the people of the North to know I'm no fiend," Kennedy told a reporter, "and did not wage war on women and children except as a matter of necessity and retaliation."[63] Finally, Kennedy admitted his part in the plot to burn New York. At six A.M. of the day he was to be executed, Kennedy confessed in the presence of the *New York Times* reporter. Because of the clear chronology of events Kennedy presents, the author has chosen to present the confession with some omissions. Headley detailed the methods used and the catalogue of burnings as well as the identities of the arsonists. It is the contrast to Kennedy's initial "confession" apparent in this last confession that is startling. Kennedy stated:

> After my escape from Johnson's island I went to Canada, where I met a number of Confederates. They asked me if I was willing to go on an expedition. I replied, "Yes, if it is in the service of my country." I was then sent to New York.... There were eight men in our party, of whom two fled to Canada.... I set fire to four places — Barnum's Museum, Lovejoy's Hotel, Tammany Hotel, and the New England House. The others only started fires in the house where each was lodging and then ran off. Had they all done as I did we would have had thirty-two fires and played a huge joke on the fire department.... There was no fiendishness about it.... I expected to die then, and If I had it would have been all right.... I wish to say that killing women and children was the last thing thought of. We wanted to let the people of the North understand that there are two sides to this war, and they can't be rolling in wealth and comfort while we in the South are bearing all the hardships and privations.[64]

Later that day, railing against the government and cursing his fate until his neck was in the noose and a hood was lowered over his head, at the last moment, Kennedy broke into song: "Trust to luck, trust to luck / Stare fate in the face / For your heart will be easy if it's in the right place."

Robert Cobb Kennedy was hanged a little after 1:15 in the afternoon, the last Confederate soldier to be executed during the Civil War. "He possessed all the attributes of a gentleman, and was sincere, true, intelligent, and absolutely fearless," John Headley wrote as a final tribute to his friend.[65]

As for Headley, undeterred and unrepentant, his work was not done. On February 2, 1865, Headley and Martin left Toronto for the United States, arrived at Cincinnati, and headed for points south, in particular, Richmond. After deciding it was not safe to remain in Cincinnati, the men went to Louisville before attempting to go to Virginia. While in Louisville they read a notice in the newspaper announcing "the arrival at the Louisville Hotel of Andrew Johnson [Lincoln's vice-president] ...." It was decided that Headley and Martin, with the aid of Confederates in the city, would kidnap the vice-president and "carry him through Virginia as a prisoner of war."[66]

After casing the hotel several times and familiarizing themselves with the layout of the upstairs rooms and the parlor, the men arranged to intercept Johnson as he came out of his room. "If you go with us quietly," they planned to say, "well and good. If you refuse, we will kill you right here."[67] Headley detailed the proposed escape with the hostage in tow: "After leaving the hotel we would drive down Main to Eighth Street, thence to Market and down to Twelfth Street, out then to Broadway and on out the Eighteenth Street road."[68]

After devising a system of signals and arranging for a carriage driver, the men went to the hotel. "I walked down the hall, passing Johnson's room slowly," Headley reported. After waiting for nine hours, only to find that "Johnson never appeared anywhere," Headley learned that Johnson "had left on a boat at 5 o'clock in the afternoon for Cincinnati. This was an hour and night of bitter disappointment.... The opportunity had been ours, perhaps, to perform a service which might have affected the destiny of our country."[69]

It is not possible to determine whether or not Headley knew of a parallel plot to kidnap President Lincoln involving Confederate agent

John Wilkes Booth and his action team in March 1865, but the Louisville scheme was certainly in keeping with the Confederacy's growing determination to capture or kill leaders of the government of the United States.

The "bitter disappointment" expressed by Headley at the failure of the kidnap plot had turned to grief over the probable fate of the Confederacy. Passing through their beloved Kentucky, stopping only to steal horses and secure passes, Headley and Martin skirted Northern encampments, posed as roving cattlemen, embraced partisan guerrillas and battled Union "bushwhackers" as they made their way to Richmond.

It was too late. When Headley's train from Danville to Richmond was unexpectedly stopped, Headley saw "a long passenger train and we soon learned that president Davis, his Cabinet and the other civil officers of the Confederate government were on board...." Martin boarded the train and spoke to Judah Benjamin, who told Martin that "General John C. Breckenridge, who was now Secretary of War, was in North Carolina with General Joseph E. Johnston." Headley reported, "Everything was now in confusion and it was an hour of consternation. Still, no one seemed to lose courage or hope."[70]

Unwilling to accept anything resembling defeat, Headley and Martin struggled to reach Lynchburg in a frantic effort to rally leaderless commands and regroup scattered, demoralized soldiers. News of Lee's surrender reached the men as they crossed the Blue Ridge Mountains and encountered Jefferson Davis and Judah Benjamin in the town of Salisbury, North Carolina, as they fled for their lives from Union authorities.

Headley recorded his impressions of both men, calling Davis' bearing "dignified but graceful ... a sort of benign and lofty simplicity that was at once inspiring and captivating." Benjamin, he wrote, was "of stout, stocky build, about five feet ten inches in height, and a strong, bright face ... and busy eyes."[71]

Following the defeated ranks to Charlotte, North Carolina, the men learned of the assassination of President Lincoln. "This news kept all busy for the time being and served to intensify a brief season of suspense."[72]

A few days later, Jefferson Davis received word from Breckenridge that "announced the surrender of all the armies by an agreement for peace with General Sherman. We realized our country was no more,"[73] Headley wrote as he and Martin, hoping to provide escort and protection to Davis, followed the President's party south to Georgia. According to Headley, he and Martin witnessed Davis, "the undaunted Chieftain of his unfortunate country, accompanied by his private secretaries and a cavalry escort, as he departed from Washington, Georgia, signaling the formal dissolution of the Confederate government. This disconsolate hour was bitter in sorrow, in desolation and in terror ... there was no contemplation now safe over the past, present, and future wreck and ruin of homes and people."[74]

And home they went, passing into Kentucky, encountering marauding bounty hunters and Federal marshals looking for Confederate criminals. Headley and Martin knew that President Johnson had issued an Amnesty Proclamation, one that did not include "All persons who have made raids into the United States from Canada."[75]

After hearing that a warrant for their arrest had been issued, Martin fled to Canada while Headley drifted toward Nebo, Kentucky, convinced he would be protected at home. "I found that a bitter feeling between neighbors still existed," he wrote, "but many Union men of my old acquaintance gave me a hearty welcome."[76] In fact some "neighbors" risked punishment for harboring Headley. To avoid capture or imprisonment, it was with some reluctance that Headley petitioned President Andrew Johnson for a pardon: "I frankly stated in the application that I had been one of the raiders from Canada and had endeavored to serve the cause of the South in every capacity ... but that none of the expeditions from Canada had been a success."[77]

While awaiting word of his pardon, Headley cautiously stayed away from his home. He finally climbed the fence to his father's home when federal soldiers, many of whom he'd known from childhood, captured him. Headley escaped through an open window as the guards waited for him to collect his baggage and fled to Tennessee. In Nashville, Headley found Martin, who "had found nothing to do as an exile in Canada"[78] was on his way home to Kentucky. Headley followed, anxious to see his fiancée, Mary Overall, who had been imprisoned for some weeks as a "disloyal" citizen. Martin was captured in Louisville, "on orders from New York."[79]

When Headley finally reached home, his mother gave him a letter from President Johnson. Headley was officially pardoned. "President Johnson proceeded gradually to discharge large numbers not yet tried, and many noted prisoners who had been confined at hard labor in penitentiaries," Headley wrote. "Among the prisoners who were in irons or close confinement and awaiting trial was Colonel Robert M. Martin, at Fort Lafayette. The President granted him an unconditional pardon" in the summer of 1866, "after a wretched confinement of about seven months."[80]

And though the plot to burn New York City terrified but did not destroy, Northern civilians would never rest easy for the remainder of the war. "What next?" some joked nervously. What *was* next? Pestilence?

FIVE

Out of Canada

"Whatever houses I may visit, I will come for the benefit of the sick, remaining free of all intentional injustice, of all mischief..."
                                        The Hippocratic Oath

"The trunk Doctor Blackburn named 'Big Number 2' will kill them at sixty yards distance."
                        Godfrey Joseph Hyams, Confederate agent*

On a balmy spring night in Bermuda, an island in a sun-washed archipelago where tales of demon visitations abounded and a deadly yellow fever epidemic claimed many lives, a portly, middle-aged American doctor walked slowly through the thatched warren that served as a hospital. With uncommon devotion, he ministered to the dead and dying: sailors, servants, well-shod travelers and orphaned indigents.

Sometimes he gently wiped sweat from fevered brows with his own clean white handkerchief or poured lemonade and bits of ice through parched lips. He held patients in his arms, cradling their heads as they vomited black bile, a sure sign the end was near. Always, the doctor tended, soothed, tried to help. It was his first trip to the island. He'd arrived in mid–April 1864 and by late June, he was more than proving his reputation as a great healer. One year later, he would receive a special humanitarian commendation from the Queen herself.

On another night, while treating yellow fever victims at the newly constructed Hamilton Hotel, a grand tourist hostelry packed with the desperately ill, Dr. Luke Pryor Blackburn insisted that nurse Dinah Amery give him extra woolen blankets to cover a female patient. She must be "sweated more," he said. "I did not think the woman required

*Benn Pitman, The Assassination of President Lincoln and the Trial of the Conspirators (Cincinnati: Moore, Wiltsach and Baldwin, 1865), p. 56.

any extra clothing, as she was sweating profusely at the time," nurse Amery later testified.[1]

But the doctor insisted, even as Amery warned him that only a few clean blankets remained; the rest, she said, were contaminated, soaked with effluvia from patients who had recently died. As the nurse looked on, the doctor wrapped the covers tightly around the sick woman "in order," he said, "to prevent the air getting to her."[2] The moment Blackburn left the hotel, nurse Amery removed the swaddling and opened a window. Soon, a gentle tropical breeze cooled the exhausted woman through the night.

When Blackburn returned the next morning to find the patient comfortable if not improved (most of the Hamilton's cases were terminal), "He seemed annoyed," the nurse reported, "and told me to come to his room.... I helped him to lift down a trunk from which he took some partly new articles of clothing "some guernseys [tight shirts], coats, trousers ... all being woolen ... [he] wrapped them tightly around the woman and other patients."[3]

Later, the nurse saw Blackburn gather the soiled bedding and clothing as well as his stained white handkerchiefs. He neatly packed them in trunks along with brand new clothing fit for a fine gentleman, a dandy or even a president. Again, Amery protested until Blackburn accused her of being "more of a doctor than a nurse," and threatened to stop her from attending other patients.[4]

And at Slater's, another hotel-turned-hospital, nurse Frances Cameron witnessed more of the doctor's disturbing methodologies. After a patient, one Captain Galloway, had expired, Blackburn was asked about the disposal of the man's clothing. "Dr. Blackburn sent Cameron out of the room.... When she returned the body was shrouded.... 'I don't know what became of the clothes,'" she later testified, adding that just before the Captain died, "he had a hoemorage [*sic*] of the lungs."[5]

Nurse Cameron watched Blackburn wipe Galloway's mouth with a white handkerchief, which, she said, later disappeared. And through the long, dark nights, the doctor worked away, soothing, always soothing. When a patient was lost, he quietly removed all traces of the terrible illness.

The disappearance of the soiled bed linens on which his patients died caused concern but no one reported these peculiar events. No one dared. After all, the doctor had risked all and come to the land of demons where disease feasted and usually won. Some weeks later, taking eight trunks

Dr. Luke Pryor Blackburn, engineer of biological warfare and later governor of Kentucky (Kentucky Historical Society).

filled with the contaminated items, the doctor left Hamilton, Bermuda, and traveled across the Atlantic on the steamer *Alpha* to Halifax, Nova Scotia, a distance of just under 800 miles. By July 12, Blackburn was in Halifax with his cargo.

There, by previous arrangement, he met Confederate operative Godfrey Joseph Hyams, an impoverished English shoemaker. According to historian Edward Steers, Hyams "emigrated from London, England, to New York City in 1852."[6] After settling in Helena, Arkansas, for several years, Hyams left the South for Toronto, "claiming that he wanted to avoid the difficulties of war."[7]

A man of dubious loyalties (he'd originally been a Union supporter), Hyams decided to support the Confederate cause because the "Yankees had insulted his wife."[8]

Blackburn ordered Hyams to ship the trunks to Boston, New Bern, North Carolina, and Washington, D.C. He emphasized the nation's capitol, boasting that the trunk he named "Big Number Two" would "kill them at sixty yards distance."[9] Hyams was then asked to sell the contents of the trunks at auctions in Washington, Norfolk and New Bern.

And, Blackburn added, for good measure, he'd infected some clothing with smallpox as well. He demanded that Hyams make sure the yellow fever clothing was distributed in a warm climate when contagion might spread more rapidly. The smallpox-infected clothing, Blackburn told Hyams, must be saved for the colder, northern climes. In return, Hyams was promised a great fortune. "He told me I should have $100,000 for my services; $60,000 of it directly after I returned to Toronto.... He said I might make ten times one hundred thousand dollars ... and offered his hand in friendship," he later testified.[10]

Aided by an officer from the *Alpha*, Hyams removed Blackburn's eight trunks and brought them to the Farmer's Hotel in Halifax. As instructed, "Hyams next took three trunks containing the doctor's personal belonging to the Halifax Hotel where he turned them over to him."[11]

Assured by Hyams that the trunks would be smuggled into the United States, Blackburn demanded that they not be opened for inspection. He told Hyams to bribe the customs officials if necessary and asked the operatives to repack the trunks before he shipped them. If Hyams had never before had yellow fever, the doctor cautioned, he must "get some camphor and chew it, and get some strong cigars, the strongest you can get, and be sure to keep gloves on when handling the things."[12]

To cover shipping, bribing of customs officials and other travel expenses, Blackburn gave Hyams 26 pieces of gold, hardly the fortune he'd been promised. And there was one more item, Blackburn told Hyams. He had packed a fine leather valise with "some very elegant dress shirts" meant as a gift for President Lincoln. "This valise I declined taking charge of," Hyams reported, "and turned it over to him [Blackburn] at the Halifax Hotel, and I afterward heard that it had been sent to the President."[13]

When Hyams demanded part of his promised payment, Blackburn told him that as soon as he had successfully gotten the trunks to the United States and distributed them in the various cities, upon his return to Canada, he was to go to Jacob Thompson and produce a bill of sale for the clothing as guarantee of their shipment. Surely then, Blackburn assured Hyams, he would be grandly compensated.

One week later, "Hyams and his cargo arrived in the Boston harbor," and "He had the trunks expressed to Philadelphia and New York." Hyams accompanied "Big Number Two" to Washington, D.C., where he sold it and other trunks for auction at W.L. Wall and Company under an assumed name, J.W. Harris. Eventually the contents of the trunks ended up in used clothing stores, a usual practice at the time.[14] According to historian Edward Steers, Jr., "Hyams now had to find a way to get the remaining trunks to Norfolk and New Bern. He was able to strike a deal with a military sutler ... who had permission to pass through the military lines to both cities."[15]

His plans in place, the attack launched according to plan, Blackburn returned to Toronto. While many Confederates were agonizing over weakened armies, lack of supplies and sinking morale, the Confederate agents in Canada were determined to fight on. Blackburn was sure his project would not fail. He told Hyams, "I want you to kill and destroy as many of the Northern army, or the people of the place you go to if you can."[16]

He might have reasoned that his unholy scheme was a just and timely solution, a punishment well deserved by the hated Yankees. He believed "an epidemic of the deadly disease would prove devastating to Northern war efforts."[17] Perhaps Blackburn had forgotten the Hippocratic Oath he was sworn to uphold: "I will use my power to help the sick to the best of my ability and judgment; I will abstain from harming or wrongdoing any man by it."

To heal the sick was his life's dream. Luke Pryor Blackburn came early and young to his calling, not yet out of his teens when he began to treat patients. According to his biographer, Nancy Disher Baird, "the absence of the doctor's private papers leaves unfortunate gaps in personal information."[18]

Much if not all was lost or destroyed by family members, so little remains of Blackburn's personal correspondence. The reasons for the dearth of materials remain a matter of speculation, but we do know that he was born on a sprawling farm in Woodford County, Kentucky, to Edward M. and Lavinia Bell Blackburn on June 16, 1816, one of "at least twelve children."[19] Today, boasts the tourist commission, Woodford is a land of "bourbon, wines and bloodlines." Blackburn's Kentucky was far wilder — a frontier with rolling plateaus, abundant game and teal-blue grasses as far as the eye could see.

His was a well-born, learned and ambitious upbringing. His paternal grandfather was a political aspirant who had hosted Marquis de Lafayette, his uncle and role model Churchill Blackburn was a world famous physician, and his maternal grandfather was a member of Kentucky's Constitutional Convention in 1799. At just 16, hoping to follow in his uncle's footsteps and convinced he would become a great healer, Blackburn was apprenticed to Churchill Blackburn just as an Asiatic cholera epidemic swept through Kentucky in 1832. He would learn well.

Painful, all-consuming and deadly, cholera was once confined to India and the Orient. In 1828, the disease ravaged Russia, Germany and the British Isles, arriving in the United States due to waves of immigrants and increased trans–Atlantic travel. At home in Kentucky, young Luke Blackburn closely studied graphic accounts of the disease and its symptoms: "Evacuation of the bowels [diarrhea], leg cramps, nausea, stomach pain ... violent headaches ... tightness in the chest ... severe pains throughout the body." As death neared and "the pulse weakened, food was vomited undigested, followed by watery phlegm. Urination ceased ... and the victim appeared as a cold, contracted, blue tinged but still living corpse."[20]

Hot weather, poor sanitation, unclean drinking water and raw sewage spread the disease. In New York City alone, "a city judged by sage ex-mayor Philip Hone to be filthier than any in Canada or Europe," cholera killed over 2,000 people in one month. Treatment was barbaric; "bleeding, cupping, purging," did nothing to save immigrant and minority victims who, unlike white, mobile residents, were unable to flee to areas with cleaner air and pure water.[21]

By the summer of 1833, cholera had come to the Bluegrass State. In spite of Kentucky's unearthly beauty, it had many contaminated wells and generally unsanitary conditions, which sent large numbers of white residents escaping the area to safety. But for those left behind, the indigent poor, enslaved blacks or town elders hoping to be spared, death often came in a little more than 24 hours.

"The houses of business were all closed and scarcely anything was to be seen or heard in the streets except the hearse bearing its victims to the grave or some terrified messenger rushing or galloping for assistance," Lexington resident J.J. Polk wrote. "If the pestilence here had any choice in its victims, it seemed to prefer the temperate ... on the other hand some of our best citizens perished."[22]

When cholera struck the town of nearby Paris, Kentucky, Blackburn and his uncle worked tirelessly to help the victims. As the young man witnessed the horrific aftermath of the epidemic — orphaned children, unburied dead and little food supply — 10 percent of the town's population was lost. It is of certain irony, an understatement, to note that Blackburn's bio-terror scheme during the Civil War was not born of a lack of first-hand experience. Rather, his knowledge of the psychological and physical devastation caused by epidemic disease was obvious.

At just 17, Blackburn completed his apprenticeship and began his formal studies at Transylvania University, a venerable Lexington, Kentucky, institution founded in 1780. When he was barely 19, Blackburn was eligible to practice medicine, having written a final thesis at Transylvania, "Cholera Maligna," in which he stated the common nineteenth century medical model: disease was a "universal sedation of organic life, manifested in the capillary tissue, then in the larger vessels and heart."[23]

Today, cholera, while still potentially deadly, is eminently treatable. "Immediate replacement of the fluid and salts lost through diarrhea" is ordered and "severe cases also require intravenous fluid replacement.... Antibiotics shorten the course and diminish the severity of the illness."[24]

As he battled the disease, Blackburn was already something of a savior, lauded as a "kind and most gentle yet bravest man ... who entered homes of the sick and dying, and many did he bring back from the jaws of death by his skill and intrepid nerve."[25]

But while his practice was well regarded, it was not lucrative (many country doctors had few patients), so Blackburn moved his wife, Ella, and son, Carey, to Natchez, Mississippi, a lusty, sprawling river city made rich by the back-breaking labor of thousands of slaves on huge cotton plantations. An expert on fine horses and well-bred cattle, Blackburn adored the place, buying and selling breeding stock, doctoring the rich and poor, managing a hospital and making friends with his neighbor, future Confederate president Jefferson Davis. And it was to this land of "King Cotton" and steamboat gambols that yellow fever came.

Because of its boggy lowlands teeming with mosquitoes, Natchez was susceptible to yellow fever, and the disease infected all manner of the population: owners of glorious mansions, "residents of the United States" who "banked in New York ... and owned land across the nation," their poorly nourished slaves, and thousands of ordinary working men and their women and children.[26]

In the nineteenth century, yellow fever was believed to be uncontrollable and highly contagious, "keeping Southerners in a state of perpetual dread."[27] It was a wasting and deadly virus known colloquially as "yellow jack," "bronze John," "black vomit," and, since it often ravaged the wet, humid South and its newcomers, was also known as the "stranger's disease." Symptoms included fever, headache, vomiting, jaundice, bleeding, delirium, seizures and, finally, coma. It had a 30 to 50 percent fatality rate and no known cure, so any outbreak of yellow fever caused panic and despair. Blackburn would become exceedingly familiar with the fever's fatal etiology, working day and night, proving, as Natchez's elected health officer, that quarantining infected patients helped to stem the epidemic. He was a hero, lauded and loved. In a few years, after having faced down "yellow jack," his knowledge would serve him all too well.

The years prior to the Civil War were both tragic and lucrative for Blackburn. In 1856, a malaria epidemic killed his wife, in spite of his round-the-clock efforts to stop the illness even as he was concluding that overuse of quinine (the common remedy) was not as effective as "replacement of body fluids, preventing dehydration," a notably modern and effective remedy in an age before antibiotic therapies and sophisticated diagnostics. At the urging of friends, the grief-stricken doctor traveled to Europe and toured hospitals. Within a year he returned to America with a new wife, Julia Churchill. When the war began, all of Blackburn's brothers and brothers-in-law immediately joined the Confederate army, "even those living in Union states."[28]

While Blackburn was "a states rightist and slaveholder," he did not enlist. Without facts, or any private correspondence, one can only speculate. Why did he not serve as a doctor for the Confederacy from the beginning? His skills would have been invaluable. Perhaps, as his biographer Nancy Baird reasoned, "his reluctance to enlist may have been due to his age (forty-five) and lack of military experience."[29]

He was not content to serve the South as a field surgeon or arms procurer and was frustrated when his suggestion to Confederate leaders in Richmond of a position of "General Inspector of Hospitals and camps ... willing to take this position without pay or rank," was ignored. He volunteered to supply blockade runners (manned seagoing vessels) that defied the Northern blockades of Southern ports by buying much needed medicines, arms and ice. It was not enough.[30]

Aflame with hatred of President Abraham Lincoln and his war machine and likely inspired by his soldier brother's vow to "hold every Union traitor as my enemy ... to see Union blood flow deep enough for my horse to swim in it," Blackburn went to Toronto, as Mississippi's agent in Canada, determined to find a magnificent and deadly opportunity. It would come within months.[31]

In the early spring of 1864, a yellow fever epidemic erupted in Bermuda. It was a perfect tactic for Blackburn: the spread of germs and the harm they could do to an unwitting civilian population. Elated, he later told Hyams his plan, "directed against the masses of Northern people solely to create death," was infallible.[32]

Immediately, he offered his services without compensation to physicians in Bermuda, a welcome and humanitarian gesture. Surely, they believed, as recipients of "yellow jack's" ferocity, that a savior was among them. Bermuda also played an important role in the Civil War. According to Judy Perry, museum guide at the Bermuda National Trust Museum at Globe House in St. George's, "In Bermuda they would load supplies onto the little blockade runner ships. Those would go from Bermuda to North Carolina and sometimes other Confederate ports being blockaded by Union ships."

Perry said that upon arrival "the blockade runners would pick up the cotton and ship it back to Britain. Britain didn't have any other supplier of cotton at that time other than the Confederate states, so they were desperate.... People were out of work in Britain due to the lack of cotton; that is why they were frantic to get it."

Frantic, perhaps, but also immensely wealthy. Money flowed through the port of St. George's, Confederate opportunists disproving Britain's "neutrality" by unloading huge cargoes of much-needed arms and supplies from the British ships the Confederacy used to run the northern blockades.

Blackburn's first trip was a success. Largely due to his efforts, the epidemic was contained in Hamilton, Bermuda, and "bronze John," in all its fury, was sent to America. In Toronto, Blackburn remained an active operative, apparently concocting a plot to poison the Croton, New York, reservoir. Reportedly, his new scheme was interrupted when security concerns dampened the Confederate's ardor and word came of a new and more terrible yellow fever epidemic, one that might abort the lucrative and necessary blockade trade between Bermuda and the coastal South.

In mid–August, Blackburn again sailed for the islands. He arrived on September 4 and was welcomed back like a sweet, cleansing wind. He went to the island of St. George's, where all the wealth and high-stepping splendor enjoyed by the number of Confederate sympathizers living there could not protect them from the "stranger's disease." The good doctor was only too glad to wipe their brows, wrap them tightly and ease their dying. As they weakened, he might have told them tales of Lee's fighting angels and the valor of Stonewall Jackson, of how their beloved South was but a step from glory.

But this time, he was being watched. When the American consul Charles M. Allen learned that Blackburn had again "refused all offers of a pecuniary nature, either for his services here or for expenses incurred by his visit," he grew wary. Perhaps it was the doctor's claim that he was desirous only of "benefiting this community, who had manifested so much sympathy for their 'Holy Cause' and never neglected to advertise on all possible occasions the cause of the rebels," that gave Allen true pause.[33]

But Blackburn stayed on, infecting more clothing and making arrangements to have additional trunks shipped to Halifax. Edward Swan, a resident of St. George's, agreed to store the trunks until the spring when final shipping arrangements could be made. It would later come back to haunt him. His second mission completed, Blackburn returned to Canada toward the end of October 1864 and "melted back into the shadowy clandestine apparatus operating from that country."[34]

While many of Blackburn's associates applauded his efforts, there is record of at least one Confederate agent in Canada engaged in the plan to kidnap or assassinate President Lincoln who questioned the morality of the bio-terror scheme. Others had warned of the impending attack, but did nothing to stop it. Two letters of uncommon importance have come to light. They must be considered chronologically as they underscore the competition among the most zealous Confederate agents to enact the perfect, infallible plan.

The first communication was from Robert E. Lee to Jefferson Davis regarding a letter from Davis and an enclosed note he'd been given in person from Benjamin Stringfellow, a trusted Confederate spy. Apparently Jefferson Davis was seeking Lee's advice on a matter of great importance, one that posed a moral dilemma (probably the Lincoln kidnap and assassination plot). The note that Davis forwarded was from Reverend Kensey Johns Stewart, an Episcopal clergyman and clandestine Confederate operative working out of Canada at the same time Blackburn was going back and forth to Bermuda. Stewart was a cousin by marriage to Robert E. Lee. His wife, Hannah Lee, was Robert E. Lee's first cousin.

> Mr. President Chaffins 25 Oct. '64
> Mr. Stringfellow has just handed me your note enclosing one from Mr. Stewart-Mr. S. [Stewart] said upon your advice he had come to consult me upon a project he had in view, especially as to its morality. I gave him opinion as far as I understood it & thought from what he said he had not determined to undertake it, but that it would depend upon an interview he would have with you....[35]

Lee went on to say that he does not know much of the work of Reverend Stewart: "I could give him no advice or recommendation as to his course — He must make up his own opinion as to what he should do...." Lee then referred to the project, one that "must be kept a profound secret.... I had inferred that his companions were to be taken from Canada, until I got a note from General Fitz [Fitzhugh] Lee, asking if he must send some half dozen of his men to Mr. S. [Stewart] ... to take a party of men from here seems to me to ensure failure & I could not recommend it...."[36]

Lee also added, "Upon reperusal of your note I perceive you ask my advice — I do not think Mr. Stuart [sic] by his habits life &c qualified for the undertaking he proposes — It was on this account that I could not advise others to join him ... and can form no opinion as to his probable success."[37]

According to historian Steers, "despite Lee's negative evaluation of Stewart's secret project, Davis approved it anyway and sent Stewart to Canada in November, 1864, with a draft for $20,000 ($500,000 today) in Confederate gold to finance his operation."[38]

While in Canada, Stewart was apparently made privy to Blackburn's yellow fever operation. On December 24, 1864, Reverend Stewart wrote to Jefferson Davis from Toronto to inform him of Blackburn's plan and object to it on moral grounds. Steers calls the letter a "smoking gun." This author wholeheartedly agrees.

Stewart began the letter by bemoaning the failure of other plots such as the burning of New York and the conspiracy taking place in Canada. He told Davis the failure of the Canadian plot was due to the operatives there and audaciously advised him to take harsh measures against his agents: "Your excellency is aware that when a Negro is slightly chastised, he hates you, but a just and thorough whipping humbles him." Stewart goes on to his own moral objections:

> I cannot regard you as capable of expecting the blessings of God upon, or being personally associated with, instruments & plans such as I describe below. As our country has been and is entirely dependent upon God, we cannot afford to displease him. Therefore it cannot be our policy to employ wicked men to destroy the persons & property of private citizens, by inhumane and cruel acts. I name only one. $100 of public money has been paid to one 'Hyams,' a shoemaker, for services rendered by conveying and causing to be sold in Washington at auction, boxes of small-pox [sic] clothing. As I name not this for the injury of the well meaning party who planned it [Blackburn].... I wish no other notice taken of it, than such things be discouraged.[39]

Stewart must have had a high regard for Blackburn because he never names him as the progenitor of the plot; rather he blames his operative, Hyams. Among other things, the letter corroborated the beliefs of historians like James O. Hall and Edward Steers, Jr., the late William Tidwell and others, that in spite of Jefferson Davis' defenders who argued that he knew nothing of the Canadian plots, the Confederate president and his Secretary of State Judah Benjamin were at least aware of Blackburn's actions as well as the Lincoln conspiracies but did nothing to stop them.

And, as Blackburn contemplated his next move, his associates in Canada were planning a bold and decisive action against President Lincoln. John Wilkes Booth arrived in Montreal on October 18, 1864, and checked into the St. Lawrence Hall Hotel, immediately meeting with Confederate operative George N. Sanders, "a Kentuckian who harbored a fanatical devotion for the Confederacy and an equally fanatical hatred for Lincoln"[40] and who, "while in Europe awaiting his confirmation as United States consul in London, advocated the assassination of Napoleon III." It is not a stretch to assume that Sanders urged Booth to do the same to Lincoln.

It is the belief of historians Steers, James O. Hall, David Winfred Gaddy, Betty J. Ownsbey and others prominent in the field of Lincoln assassination research that at the very least, final plans for the abduction of Lincoln were formed at that time. An earlier effort to kidnap Lincoln had failed. It would not be allowed to happen again.

During the times Blackburn was collecting infected clothing in Bermuda (the end of April and again in August 1864), a Confederate agent from Virginia named Thomas Nelson Conrad was infiltrated into Washington, D.C. Familiar with the city and Lincoln's movements, Conrad planned to capture the President as he traveled back and forth to his summer White House on the grounds of the Old Soldier's Home on the outskirts of Washington: "We had determined to capture the carriage and take possession of Mr. Lincoln, and then whether to move with him through Maryland to the lower Potomac [Charles County in Southern Maryland]."[41] Judah Benjamin financed Conrad's mission from funds approved by Jefferson Davis. The infamous guerrilla Colonel John S. Mosby was directed to "aid and facilitate the movements of Conrad."[42]

Accompanied by three operatives who stationed themselves in Lafayette Square in front of the White House, Conrad decided he had to move quickly. It was well known that Lincoln and his family escaped the typhoid-ridden city to the high grounds of the summer White House, and because fall was approaching, Lincoln would not make the trip again for many months. All was at the ready.

Conrad saw that cavalry accompanied the usually unescorted presidential carriage. Perhaps this was the work of other Confederates pursuing the same end, but thwarting Conrad's plot. It is more likely that Lincoln's devoted advisors insisted he have more protection as threatening letters, ignored by a bemused Lincoln and stuffed into a file labeled "assassination," continued to pour into the White House. Conrad aborted the mission, stating fatuously in his memoirs that "had Lincoln fallen into the meshes of the silken net we had spread for him, he would never have been the victim of the assassin's heartless, bloody and atrocious crime."[43]

Within days, some Confederate commissioners made a secret trip to the Confederate capitol, presumably to plan and orchestrate another kidnap or assassination plot. After meeting with Jefferson Davis and his cousin Robert E. Lee, Brigadier General Edwin Gray Lee returned to Canada with an allocation of $20,000 from Jefferson Davis.

By the end of September, John Wilkes Booth began to recruit a team to help him capture Lincoln. Booth was an ideal operative, a native Marylander, who had been involved in obtaining and smuggling quinine to ailing Confederate prisoners early in the war. His celebrity (he is often compared to Tom Cruise by Ford Theatre historians) and his frequent appearances throughout the North and South allowed him to move though the lines with impunity.

Feted, adored, bright and completely committed to the cause of the wounded South, he recruited two boyhood friends, Michael O'Laughlen and Samuel Arnold, both smart, young and dedicated Confederate soldiers. By January, Booth had assembled the remainder of his action team. It is now believed that Lewis Thornton Powell, the young soldier responsible for the nearly fatal attack on Secretary of State William A. Seward, had been sent to Booth from Colonel John Mosby's ranks. David Herold, a young, college-educated druggist's assistant from Washington, who was familiar with every byway and cranny in southern Maryland, George Atzerodt, a German immigrant and Confederate boatman, and Judah Benjamin's operative and dispatch carrier John Harrison Surratt completed the team. Surratt's mother, Mary E. Surratt, would hang for her role in the assassination conspiracy.

While it is not the goal of the present author to illuminate the complex and well-researched aspects of the Lincoln assassination, ably interpreted by the authors of *Blood on the Moon, His Name is Still Mudd, Come Retribution, The Lincoln Murder Conspiracies, Alias "Paine," April '65* and others, it is compelling to view the progression of events orchestrated by Canadian agents and the Davis government during the last months of the war. Each operative knew what the other had plotted, no matter what rivalries existed, no matter what the outcome.

At no time did any of the men betray each other. Only Godfrey Hyams, thought to have been a double agent by some historians, exposed some of the plots and was viewed as a turncoat by loyal Confederates. It is the opinion of these scholars that if the Lincoln schemes failed, a plan to decapitate the government by assassination or the use of explosives was the primary focus of the last months of the war.

To achieve that end, there was a major power shakeup in Canada. Jacob Thompson, the head of Confederate operations there, was replaced and a new order was established. It was not unexpected. As Reverend Kensey Johns Stewart indicated in his letter to Jefferson Davis, "Colonel T. [Thompson] has acquired much information and adopted excellent plans but God has been against him. *Everything has failed by divine intervention*" [Stewart's emphasis]. While couching Thompson's firing with diplomatic grace, Confederate Secretary of State Judah Benjamin's communication to him in the waning days of December 1864 was definitive:

> I have now to inform you that from reports which reach us from trustworthy sources we are satisfied that so close espionage is kept upon you that your services have been deprived of the value which is attached to your further residence in Canada. The president thinks, therefore, that as soon as the gentleman arrives who bears this letter ... it will be better that you transfer to him as quietly as possible all of the information that you have obtained and the release of funds in your hands and then return to the Confederacy.[44]

"The 'gentleman' was Brigadier General Edwin Gray Lee," formerly of the Second Virginia Infantry and temporary commander of the Stonewall Brigade.[45] He was a second cousin to Robert E. Lee (his father Edmund was Robert E. Lee's first cousin), a lawyer, a poet and, at 28, a seasoned soldier dangerously ill with a chronic lung disease.

Whether his transfer from command in the field to command of Confederate operatives in Canada was because of precarious health (the doctors at Richmond recommended a cold, dry climate where he could live comfortably with nothing to harass him) or by clandestine design, he met with Judah Benjamin in Richmond twice in one day and Secretary of War William A. Seddon "morning & night" before leaving for Canada.[46]

The journey was long and arduous and taxed the ailing young man. After running the Union blockade at Wilmington, North Carolina, with the ship "rolling like a tub," Edwin Lee reached Nassau, relieved to inform Secretary of War Judah P. Benjamin "Good fortune attended me all the way to Richmond, and we were able to come out so rapidly that I had no opportunity of advising you when I should leave Wilmington or by what vessel...." General Edwin Gray Lee arrived in Halifax, Nova Scotia, on December 30, 1864.[47]

Lee's Canadian diary chronicles much of his stay in Canada, its pages made remarkable by missing entries (especially around the time of the assassination), accounts of his leisure time, fishing, attending the theatre, bursts of patriotic sentiment and increasingly frail health. The young general was dying by degrees, fighting to complete his mission. When Edwin Lee reached Toronto, he met with Jacob Thompson and gave him Secretary Benjamin's dispatch:

> This letter will be delivered to you by Brig. Genl. E.G. Lee who is especially recommended to you by the President as meriting your entire and unreserved confidence. I have stated to Genl. Lee many things which could not well be committed to paper, and he will give you full information of my views which, in this instance, are but the reflex of those of the President.... The President supposes that you may desire to return home....[48]

As Thompson prepared to leave Canada, Secretary Benjamin "wrote to ascertain whether Thompson fully understood his previous instructions to pay over to Lee $20,000 to be used by Lee at his discretion."[49] It is of interest to note that Lee and his wife, Sue, stayed with Reverend Kensey Johns Stewart while in Toronto. "Dr. Stewart ... had married Hannah Lee, Edwin's mother."[50]

On March 10, Edwin Lee's diary notes an important event. Lee was moving his base to Montreal, the very heart of the Confederate clandestine network. Before Lee left Toronto, he honored a day decreed by President Davis to be one of "fasting, humiliation and prayer observed by us all."[51]

Lee's host, Reverend Kensey Johns Stewart, led the services before Lee and his wife left for Montreal and the palatial St. Lawrence Hall hotel, the center of Confederate operations. "Inside the handsome entrance hall was a reading room on one side, with a large bar on the other." The hotel had a post office, a "circulating" library, "a telegraph bureau and a barbershop ... the only hotel in the Canadas [*sic*] whose bar served mint juleps."[52]

Picturing the bustle and elegance of the St. Lawrence Hall, the grand rooms and gourmet dining, and, in the thick of it, Confederates sipping familiar drinks and planning the demise of a president and his government is intriguing to say the least. And on at least one occasion in Montreal Dr. Luke Blackburn treated Edwin Lee during his stay. Lee's fatal lung condition appears to

Brigadier General Edwin Gray Lee, CSA, Jacob Thompson's replacement in Canada (courtesy of the Museum of the Confederacy, Richmond Virginia).

have been due to chronic infection, if not tuberculosis. Lee's diary entry of March 30, 1865 states, "Dr. Blackburn put an [word illegible] in my breast." Most likely this was a drain of some sort to alleviate congestion or release mucous or pus. Lee's biographer, Alexandra Lee Levin, refers to Dr. Blackburn as "his" physician. In spite of his consuming frailty, Edwin Gray Lee labored to facilitate and handle covert operators.

On October 19, 1864, 20 Confederate soldiers wearing civilian clothes under their uniforms crossed the Canadian border into the little town of St. Alban's, Vermont, with the goal of taking over the town, burning property and robbing banks. Their leader, Lieutenant Bennett H. Young, was, at 20, a hardened veteran who had ridden with the cavalry raider General John H. Morgan. After Morgan's death in Tennessee, his band of prison escapees fled to Canada. There, at the urging of Confederate agent Clement Claiborne Clay, a raid was made "that had produced alarm in all the towns in the United States, from Maine to Minnesota. This was the condition which was desired by the Confederates."[53]

The men arrived in St. Alban's and secured hotel rooms while Lieutenant Young, accompanied by a few of his men, cased the banks. At three in the afternoon, the band formed in the main street, tore off their civilian clothes, drew their guns and "proclaimed that they took possession of St. Alban's in the name of the Confederate States."[54]

Amid the mayhem that ensued, one citizen was killed and $200,000 dollars was taken from various banks as many of the town's residents were held at gunpoint. Within minutes, however, people poured into the streets along with Union soldiers. Snipers fired on the Confederates as they smashed vials of Greek fire against houses, barns, haystacks and the town's main bridge. In spite of the angry crowd of pursuers, Young and his men re-crossed the border and disappeared into Canada. "A gross outrage has been committed, in a peaceful and thriving village," announced a dispatch to the *Montreal Gazette* by the Vermont authorities. "It is the first duty of the government and the people of Canada to see that the right of asylum which their soil affords is not thus betrayed and violated."

The officially neutral Canadian government apprehended the raiders and recovered most of the money "but these actions did not calm the fears or reduce the anger of the Northern States who saw in it hostility to the Northern cause."[55] Americans were ordered to invade Canada in search of the raiders. President Lincoln's revocation of the invasion order averted an international incident that he believed would only help the South.

The raiders were arrested by Canadian authorities and sent to Montreal for trial. Even the terms of the Webster-Ashburton Treaty, which provided for a mutual exchange of prisoners, were denied, according to Edwin Gray Lee's biographer Alexandra Lee Levin. The raiders remained in Canada.

During the Confederate-financed trial, according to Levin, Lieutenant Bennett young "testified that whatever had been done at St. Alban's was intended to retaliate in some measure for the barbarous atrocities of Grant, Butler, Sherman ... and other Yankee officers." On December 14,

1864, because of a lack of jurisdiction, the prisoners were discharged. Outrage followed in the United States and extradition of the raiders was demanded. "U.S. army commanders were ordered to pursue the raiders into Canada and return them to New York for trial under martial law."[56] The raiders were arrested again while Richmond communicated that the soldiers were acting under orders.

Edwin Gray Lee's diary made note of the following: "Upon deciding that they should not be extradited for robbery, they were at once arrested on two other charges." Lee visited the raiders in prison and posed for pictures with the men outside the jail. When the men were sent to Toronto to be tried for "breach of neutrality," says Levin, "all other charges were withdrawn."[57]

Of greater importance is Lee's handling of Lincoln conspirator John Surratt. Known variously as "Armstrong," "Charley" and "Watson" in Lee's diaries (later verified by James O. Hall), Surratt carried Lee's all-important dispatches back to Judah Benjamin in Richmond on numerous occasions. As Surratt came and went from Canada, the news from Richmond was grim.

Lee's diary entry of April 3, 1865, read, "First news of the fall of Richmond! God help us." And on April 6, 1865, another entry stated, "Letter by Charley [Surratt] from Mr. Benjamin; my last rec'd all safe." The last clandestine projects of the war had been activated.

On or about March 31, Surratt had met with Judah Benjamin, Colonel John Mosby and possibly Jefferson Davis in Richmond. He returned to Canada with a "warrant for $1,500 in gold from the Confederate Secret Service account" and reported to Edwin Lee. A few days later, Thomas Harney, the Torpedo Bureau's explosive's expert, left Richmond and headed for Washington, D.C., and the Lincoln White House.

After the assassination, Edwin Lee "handled" John Surratt throughout his entire time as a fugitive in Canada. He moved him from safe house to safe house until his escape from Canada. "Charley leaves Quebec today," Lee's diary noted on September 16, 1865.

Several months earlier, as word of the Confederacy's imminent demise spread throughout Canada, many of the operatives knew they could not leave anytime soon, if ever. Not Luke Blackburn. He believed his name would never be linked to the Canadian cabals, so he made plans to go home, hoping to hear, in the words of a childish ditty, that "Yellow jack had grabbed them up and taken them all away."

Blackburn must have been heartened to hear that yellow fever had killed over 800 soldiers in New Bern, North Carolina, but there were no reports of widespread epidemics in Northern cities. And, surely, as news of Lee's surrender reached Canada, he grieved the lost "glory of a noble and suffering people."[58]

Confederate engineer William W. Blackford, listening to Robert E. Lee bid farewell to his troops, said, "Grim, bearded men threw themselves on the ground, covered their faces with their hands and wept like children. Officers of all ranks made no attempt to conceal their feelings, but sat on their horses and cried aloud...."[59]

Still in Canada, Luke Pryor Blackburn was horrified to learn he could not, like a dutiful soldier, make the long journey home.

On April 5, 1865, Godfrey Hyams went to the office of the American consul in Toronto with incriminating information about Confederate plots. In a lengthy statement, he told the authorities about a bomb factory "located in Toronto where Confederate agents were making a special type of explosive device," a bomb made to resemble a lump of coal that "was designed to be mixed with real coal ... eventually to make their way into furnaces or boilers."[60] When Hyams revealed the location of several of the bombs, which were "hidden beneath the floorboards of the house ... Hyams' credibility was established when the police took up the floor boards and found several explosive devices just as Hyams had claimed."[61]

Angling for a large reward, sure he would be granted immunity from prosecution for this invaluable information, Hyams then revealed, in full detail, Dr. Blackburn's yellow fever plot: "He told me I would get more honor and glory to my name than General Lee ... to destroy the army and everybody in the country." Hyams went on in exhausting detail, adding "that all the goods, he told me, had been carefully infected in Bermuda with yellow fever, smallpox and other infectious diseases...."[62]

On "Black Friday," April 14, the day Lincoln was murdered, Bermuda authorities reported that an unidentified Confederate agent told them that trunks of infected items were still in Bermuda and "alleged that some of the gentlemen connected with the office of the United States Government in Bermuda were cognizant of the matter."[63]

Hyams also added that the trunks were still in St. George's in the keep of Edward Swan. Immediately, Swan, the "lodging house keeper's" home was raided. An inquiry was ordered and Swan was charged with "having on his premises a nuisance in the shape of the Trunks in question dangerous to the health of the town." The trunks were found to contain "dirty flannels and drawers evidently taken from a sickbed ... some poultices and many other things which could have been placed there for no legitimate purpose."[64]

The *Bermuda Royal Gazette*, referring to the "Soiled Clothes Investigation in St. George's" and the clothing "impregnated with yellow fever," recorded much of the proceedings. Swan, the terrified innkeeper, was put on the stand when the hearing commenced on "Easter Tuesday in the remarkably small and inconvenient Police Court under the Town Hall in St.George's."[65]

Of course, Swann claimed to have no knowledge of the contents of the trunks. The *Bermuda Royal Gazette* reported that "Great anxiety was displayed about the Trunks by gentlemen of the Confederate office."[66]

While there is no record of who the "gentlemen" might have been, it is obvious that additional Confederate operatives had knowledge of the plot. Health officers were questioned, and one revealed that he had found "articles bearing dark stains" like "black vomit" among the clothing in the trunks. Nurses Amery and Cameron were deposed, and they related details of the doctor's suspicious behavior.[67]

Later in the proceedings, Swan admitted that Blackburn eventually told him that "the object of his mission was the destruction of the Northern masses" and demanded that the trunks be shipped to the United States in June, two months after the Lincoln assassination. Swan was "found guilty of being a nuisance" and charged with violating Bermuda's health violations. He was sentenced to four months in prison.[68]

On May 19, Blackburn was arrested in Montreal. A preliminary hearing concluded that he would be held for trial on "violating Canada's neutrality act." Bail was set at $8,000.[69]

Hyams was the first witness and testified in full detail on his association with Blackburn. The prosecution "dropped a bombshell into the trial when it introduced a deposition from William W. Cleary, Jacob Thompson's secretary, one of Jefferson Davis' key agents in Montreal."[70] Cleary told the court that Blackburn had hired Hyams to distribute the trunks; the evidence against Blackburn (as well as the Davis government) was extremely damaging.

Remarkably, despite the pile of circumstantial but incriminating evidence against him, Blackburn was acquitted of "violating Canada's neutrality act on the grounds that there was no proof that the trunks had ever been on Canadian soil."[71] But it was not over.

This information was promptly forwarded to Advocate General Joseph Holt, who was busy amassing evidence against not only the Lincoln conspirators but against Jefferson Davis and his Canadian cabals. In the miasma of shock and mourning following Lincoln's death, the United States authorities were convinced they could "Hang Jeff Davis from a sour apple tree."[72] Blackburn's capture would at least prove that Davis and company went far beyond the bounds of a "civil war."

During the trial of the Lincoln conspirators, Hyams replicated his testimony. He finally received some compensation, not from Confederate agents in Canada, but from the United States government. During June and July 1865, the Bureau of Military Justice paid him a total of $1200.10, surely not the fortune he'd been promised by Blackburn, but quite a hefty sum for the time.[73]

Luke Pryor Blackburn's extradition, however, was not a government priority because at the time there was not enough evidence to prove that Blackburn was given the okay by Jefferson Davis for bio-terrorism. And as recent research has revealed, this was not the case as proven by the letter of Kensey Johns Stewart to Jefferson Davis. According to Edward Steers, Jr., "Had the U.S. government been more diligent it might have found the evidence it sought to confirm Blackburn's activities, and also prove Jefferson Davis' knowledge and sanction of the yellow fever plot."[74]

American newspapers trumpeted news of Blackburn, who was called "The Yellow Fever Fiend" and "Dr. Black Vomit." He was also called "a hideous devil" responsible for "one of the most fiendish plots ever concocted by the wickedness of man." A final salvo blamed Blackburn for an outbreak of yellow fever in New Bern, North Carolina, and held him "responsible for the mass murder of women and children."[75]

While yellow fever epidemics occurred regularly, it was not due to Blackburn's efforts. It is now known that yellow fever is a viral disease spread by the bite of a mosquito, commonly the Aedes aegypti or Haemogogus variety. (Proven as fact by Dr. Walter Reed in 1900.)

The bloodlust was sated with the hanging of the four Lincoln conspirators. Calls to hang Blackburn faded away, but the murder charge stuck. Blackburn stayed in Canada, nursing his gravely wounded reputation and awaiting a pardon. None came.

In September 1867, yellow jack ravaged New Orleans and Galveston. Blackburn wrote to President Andrew Johnson: "From the dispatch today I see that the fever is prevailing in New Orleans, Galveston and other points to a most fatal extent.... I have had much experience in the treatment of this disease and feel confident I could render essential service to my suffering and dying countrymen...."[76]

Even though the United States consul in Toronto assured Johnson that the doctor had taken an oath of allegiance to the United States, Blackburn did not receive a reply. With a murder charge still pending against him, he returned to his beloved South in 1873 to heal the victims of "the stranger's disease." He was not arrested. Instead, many Louisville residents welcomed him as a hero. He took that sentiment to heart as he pondered the next phase of his life.

The luck of Blackburn did not pass to a like-minded man of letters who, like Blackburn, had hoped to terrify the North by any means necessary. Like Blackburn's "infallible plan solely to create death," Richard Sears McCulloh's weapon seemed a salvation.

Six

"Terror and Consternation"

"The north had become to me as a foreign land…"
Professor Richard Sears McCulloh*

"The Confederacy is *mired*. It may struggle out, for it has the fury
and the energy of a mad cat…"
Diarist George Templeton Strong†

Professor Richard Sears McCulloh had always loved cats, the feel of
their fur under his hands, the gaze of their sharp, bright eyes. Perhaps
now he steeled himself for what he was about to do. Confined to a small
room at his Richmond lab, cats of all shapes and sizes were pacing to and
fro. As a delegation of Confederate congressmen in secret session peered
through the small, glass window in the door, professor Richard Sears
McCulloh produced "a phial containing a colorless fluid, and said, if
thrown from the gallery of the House of Representatives in Washington,
it would kill every member on the floor in five minutes." Through the
window, "the committee saw that the vial having been upset, the result
predicted was accomplished…. The chemist then placed a handkerchief
on the mantle and after a given interval of time it took fire of its own
accord…. The experiments were completely satisfactory…."[1]

Confederate congressmen Williamson Simpson Oldham of Texas
and Waldo Porter Johnson of Missouri witnessed the experiment and
reported the results to President Jefferson Davis.

RICHMOND, February 11, 1865.
His Excellency Jefferson Davis, President C.S.A.
Sir — When Senator Johnson of Missouri and myself waited on you a

*Richard McCulloh to John McCulloh, 29 November 1885. McCulloch family archives
(unpublished).*
†Allan Nevins and Milton Thomas Halsey, eds. The Diary of George Templeton Strong
(New York: Macmillan, 1952). The Civil War, vol. 3, p. 381.*

few days since in relation to the prospect of annoying and harassing the enemy by means of burning their shipping, towns ... there were several remarks made by you upon the subject, that I was not fully prepared to answer, but which upon subsequent conference with parties proposing the enterprise, I find cannot apply as objections to the scheme.

1. The combustible material consists of several preparations and not one alone; and can be used without exposing the party using them to the least danger of detection whatever. The preparations are not in the hands of McDaniel, but are in the hands of Professor McCullough [*sic*], and are known but to him and one other party, as I understand.

2. There is no necessity for sending persons in the military service into the enemy's country; and in most cases the work might be done by agents, and in most cases by persons ignorant of the facts, and therefore innocent agents.

I have seen enough of the effects that can be produced to satisfy me that in most cases without any danger to the parties engaged, and in others but very slight, we can 1. Burn every vessel that leaves a foreign port for the United States. 2. We can burn every transport that leaves the harbor of New York or other Northern port with supplies for the armies of the enemy in the South; 3. Burn every transport and gunboat on the Mississippi River, as well as devastate the country of the enemy, and fill his people with terror and consternation.

I am, respectfully, your obedient servant,

W. S. OLDHAM

President Davis responded within a few days:

Secretary of State [Benjamin], at his convenience, please see General Harris [Thomas A. Harris] and learn what plan he has for overcoming the difficulty heretofore experienced.

    20 Feb'y 65
Rec'd Feb'y 17, 1865

JD[2]

In the last weeks of the war, a prominent Columbia University physics and chemistry professor became one of the dying Confederacy's last hopes. Richard Sears McCulloh turned his back on the prestige and comfort of a hard-won post to join the Confederate cause. It was wholly unexpected to many.

On September 25, 1863, shortly after the deadly draft riots in New York City, Columbia College president Charles King opened a letter that might as well have contained a bomb:

Richmond, Virginia, Sept 25, 1863

Gentlemen,

I hereby resign the Chair I have held at Columbia College.

It should encite [*sic*] no surprize [*sic*] that one, born and reared a south-erner, prefers to cast his lot with that of the South.

Permit me to thank you for all the generosity & consideration you have for nine years extended to me; and to assure you that I have always endeavored to justify the same, by zealous devotion to duty.

I shall ever cherish the kindest remembrances of the Trustees, Faculty & students of Columbia College & wish it prosperity & usefulness.

Everything in the Physical Department will be found in order.

A small a/c of Chester & Co for acids &c. is the only outstanding bill.

Apparatus ordered of M. Duboscq of Paris, will be forwarded by Samuel Haskell & Co who have been in the habit of importing for the college.

Very truly Your Obt. Sert.

R.S. McCulloh[3]

This was no common resignation born of petty grievances. In the eyes of Columbia's trustees, Richard Sears McCulloh was a traitor. And

Professor Richard Sears McCulloh, Confederate chemical weapons maker (courtesy of Richard and Anna McCulloch).

worse, his defection was widely publicized in the North at a time when Columbia's reputation was shaky at best. Some of the city's most committed unionists rightly suspected several Columbia trustees of being "doughfaces" or Copperheads (Northerners with southern principles or sympa-thies).[4]

While it was alleged that some of the Columbia trustees held Copperhead views, others such as professors John Torrey and John Jay, Columbia presi-dent King, and New York diarist George Templeton Strong were fierce opponents of slavery and fully committed to the Union cause.

Strong vented his spleen at McCulloh's defection:

Sunday, October 11, 1863

Professor McCulloh of Columbia College has sent in his resignation, dated Richmond, Virginia!!! He "has gone over to the dragons" and we are well rid of him. He has probably been offered a high price to come south and take charge of some military laboratory. What a pity this sneak did not desert six months sooner, when poor George F. Allen was still with us and Woolcott Gibbs had not gone to Boston![5]

Strong's rage was well founded. In 1854, his close friend, chemistry professor Woolcott Gibbs, lost a protracted battle for a coveted Columbia chair because he was a Unitarian in a bastion of Episcopal college trustees. The trustees knew that Gibbs was the right man for the job, but because the majority suspected him to be godless, Richard Sears McCulloh, a man of lesser qualifications, got the position.

After McCulloh's defection, the enraged trustees refused to accept McCulloh's resignation. Instead they expunged McCulloh's name from the faculty record. American statesman and Columbia trustee Hamilton Fish officially documented Columbia's stand on the McCulloh matter:

> Whereas, Richard S. McCulloh, professor of Mechanics and Physics in this college, has abandoned his post and gone to the city of Richmond and allied himself to those in rebellion against the government of the United States, therefore:
> Resolved, that the said Richard S. McCulloh is hereby expelled from the Professorship aforesaid, and that the said Professorship be and is hereby declared to be vacant.
> Resolved, that the name of Richard S. McCulloh be stricken from the list of Professors of this college, and a note stating the fact and ground of his expulsion be appended to his name.
> Hamilton Fish, Chairman[6]

It was later learned that McCulloh had gone to join the Confederate Nitre and Mining Bureau as a consulting chemist. Organized in 1862, the Bureau was in charge of mining the elements of explosives and extracting the saltpeter (nitre) to make the black powder that charged the guns, cannons and land mines. "Everywhere about the environs of Richmond could be seen large earthen ricks and heaps which contained dead horses and other animals, designed for use in the manufacture of nitre."[7]

Because "the need for specialists increased"[8] as the war continued, many Nitre and Mining Bureau scientists were given actual commissions in the first two years of the war. McCulloh probably expected to be similarly rewarded. He was not.

Much to his dismay, he remained without the commission he would have been awarded had he been appointed to the Confederacy's "scientific arm." This lack of military rank was a source of consternation for McCulloh throughout the rest of his service for the Confederacy. A commission meant status as a uniformed officer and protection under the codes of war. To remain a private citizen involved in secret work carried greater risk, especially if he should be arrested for any reason.[9]

A life of high danger did not seem characteristic of the Richard Sears McCulloh of biographical record, even as he moved restlessly from post to post. But like many men involved in clandestine work for the Confederacy, there is no personal correspondence extant to illuminate or justify his reasons for taking such a dangerous position, no postwar memoirs to explain his motivations, just evidence of a brilliant career completely changed by a violent historical episode.

Born on March 18, 1818, to James William McCulloh and Abigail Hall Sears in Baltimore, Richard McCulloh and his siblings, John, Mary Louisa, Eliza Ann, Isabella and James, roamed the large family farm, which had fine cattle and Arabian horses. Education of the male McCullohs was a must and young Richard, the darling of the family, passed easily through the University of Maryland and the College of New Jersey with a concentration in mathematics and chemistry.

Professor Richard Sears McCulloh in Parris, circa 1852 (courtesy of Richard and Anna McCulloch).

Good things followed for Richard McCulloh, the stuff proud papas boast about to neighbors and colleagues: a college preparatory program in Philadelphia and a year at the University of Maryland. He began as a sophomore at the College of New Jersey and graduated in 1836 at the age of 18. Mentored by Joseph Henry, the highly regarded chemist credited with inventing the electric motor, McCulloh was "one of three persons charged with the examinations of the Allegany summit of the Chesapeake and Ohio Canal, made with a view to ascertain whether the requisite supply of water can be commanded."[10]

Before 1840, McCulloh "held the post of Observer in the Magnetic Observatory of Girard College, Philadelphia."[11] In 1841, at the age of 23, he was appointed professor of Natural Philosophy, Mathematics and Chemistry at Jefferson College, in Canonsburg, Pennsylvania.[12]

McCulloh's elation at the appointment is obvious in a letter to his sister: "I was born to calculate, to measure stars and to pry into the chemical properties of matter."[13]

But without explanation, McCulloh changed his mind, and expressed a wish to study in Germany — not an uncommon desire for ambitious young pedants of the day — and in September 1843 resigned his university post. He changed his mind yet again and went to work at the U.S. Mint in Philadelphia as an assayer and refiner in April 1846. He was intrigued with the principals of alchemy (an early form of chemistry, tinged with magic that proposed to turn base metals into gold), so his position seemed ideal.

On December 15, 1845, he married Mary Stewart Vowell of Alexandria, Virginia, a cousin of Robert E. Lee. A daughter, Margaretta Grace Brown McCulloh, was born in 1846.

But the ever restive McCulloh again had difficulties, both personal and professional, at the mint. According to Milton Thomas Halsey, "He served until April 1, 1849, when he was abruptly displaced.... The problems were partly of a political and partly of a scientific nature.... "The influx of California gold had seriously taxed the capacity of the mint, and about the time he was removed, McCulloh had perfected a more rapid method of refining gold by the use of zinc...."[14] Perhaps this innovative method and McCulloh's desire to obtain an exclusive patent for his process caused his dismissal.

Undaunted and still hungry for recognition, McCulloh published numerous scientific pamphlets during this period. His chemical analyses of sugars and molasses, a speedier method of refining gold by the use of zinc, and "A Plan of Organization for the Naval Observatory" were but some of his projects. With scientist James Curtis Booth he contributed to the *Encyclopedia of Chemistry*.[15]

In 1849, he was unanimously named Professor of Natural Philosophy (Biology), at Princeton University, a far less contentious affair than his bitterly contested position at Columbia years later. The first few years of his tenure appeared to be relatively calm. He lectured, tended lovingly to a rose garden, and grew strawberries, but within five years, he was off to another post.

On April 3, 1854, McCulloh was elected Professor of Natural and Experimental Philosophy and Chemistry at Columbia College. George Templeton Strong attended McCulloh's inaugural address on December 3. He was not impressed:

> McCulloh is a feeble and washed out kind of man; but I did not think it possible that he could deliver so deplorably commonplace, incoherent and imbecile a piece of maundering as that which he bestowed on us. It was shameful to hear a man we have entrusted with the teaching of all that vast group of sciences to which we have committed the education of our students in knowledge of the material works of God defiling his awful subject by the utterance of trivialities and platitudes so slovenly and contemptible.[16]

Strong reported that McCulloh drilled his students into bored submission ("don't wonder the students hate him"), made dull speeches and requested extravagant amounts of money for equipment, even though, Strong added, "when unpacking nice new optical apparatus, there was certainly an air of life about the place."[17]

Reverend Morgan Dix, New York diarist, rector of Trinity Church, Columbia trustee and the son of General John A. Dix, whose troops quelled the draft riots in New York, observed McCulloh examining the senior class: "The subjects were Galvanism, Electricity, Architecture and the Steam-Engine. The examination was, on the whole, by far the most interesting that I have yet been present at, owing to the merciless and remorseless style in which it was conducted. No one was spared." In another entry, Dix was horrified to see "a class so thoroughly mauled. He showed them no kind of mercy...."[18]

On the stern and unbending professor went, in spite of the criticisms of colleagues. It seemed not to matter until the war, when everything changed. The exact reasons for McCulloh's defection may never be known but a stirring in the blood of a native Marylander living in "Yankee land" and anxious to do his part, might have been part of the equation.

But according to McCulloh family lore, the reasons for McCulloh's desertion at Columbia required little analysis. Allegedly he refused to sign an unofficial, university-based loyalty oath during the week of the draft riots. As a native Marylander, McCulloh also expressed sympathy for the Confederate cause as the conflict in New York and on the battlefields worsened. According to John McCulloh, his brother left for a previously planned vacation in Virginia and never returned to Columbia.[19]

McCulloh's sister-in-law, Anna (wife of McCulloh's brother John), founder of the Oldfields School in Glencoe, Maryland, wrote part of the family version of the professor's Confederate war service and his motivations for doing so: "A certain sort of gallantry—of self-devotion, such as led him to throw himself into the southern cause, and give up one of the best professorships in the country for it, which made him always look after unprotected women, children, and led to a certain high grace of manner felt by many, and often by myself as out of time."[20]

In 1899, John McCulloch summarized his brother's war record:

> My brother Richard served on the southern side with the rank of Lieut. Col. and was made a consulting engineer over all the works of the Confederacy, and also did the work of a scout and pioneer, making reports of the enemy's position as aide de camp on the battlefield. And when the war ended he was making his way to Cuba in a lifeboat with others and was driven by a storm into Cape Sable and was captured and made a prisoner of war and kept in the infamous Libby prison for one year. Twice he attempted to escape through the swamps of western Florida. Twice he was captured, and then released on parole.[21]

According to Glencoe school archivist Meg Gallucci, John McCulloh's partisan sensibilities were well known: "His blindness interfered with his career as did the fact that he was a Confederate sympathizer."[22]

A letter dated May 2, 1861, to Anna McCulloh from her brother, Austin, in Baltimore, underscores hatreds felt by many in Maryland shortly after the Civil War began: "Of political affairs I have no heart to write—adept at sham or claptrap and all—patriotism is that under the rule that anomalous compound of sot-craven harlequin ... who could put such a creature at its head. The country now paying the penalty...."

I can fancy nothing much worse than forced submission to black Republican despotism...."[23]

Submission to Republican despotism was clearly not acceptable to Richard Sears McCulloh as he prepared to depart for Richmond. George Templeton Strong questioned his sanity:

> From all I have heard of McCulloh's movements up to the time he left New York in July (at the end of riot week) and of his general style of talk before that time I incline to suspect he may be deranged. He has expressed no sympathy with the Rebellion, and has uttered nothing worse than moderate Copperheadism, and he has declared himself unfavorable to slavery, and in favor of gradual emancipation. It is hard therefore to account for his giving up an assured position here and casting his lot with the beggared conspirators of the south, unless we assume that he was cracked. He always seemed eccentric and queer.[24]

According to historians Alan Nevins and Milton Halsey Thomas, editors of George Templeton Strong's diary, "The more patriotic citizens of New York correctly felt that Copperhead denunciations of the draft act, and Copperhead demands for peace, were largely responsible for the riots."[25]

George Templeton Strong also suspected McCulloh's involvement: "Professors Joy and Torrey were right in supposing this ill visaged caitiff to have something to do with getting up the Riots of July '63, and that he was a secret agent of secession."[26]

In the heat of the bloody violence, Columbia trustee and famed botanist Professor John Torrey also witnessed a mob surrounding Columbia College President King's home:

> The mob wanted to burn President King's house, as he was rich and a decided republican. They barely desisted when addressed by Catholic priests. The furious bareheaded and coatless men assembled under windows and shouted aloud.... Towards evening the mob, furious as demons, went yelling over to the Colored-Orphan Asylum a little below where we live — rolling a barrel of kerosene in it, the whole structure was soon in a blaze, a smoking ruin.

After three long days, Torrey reported, "Just as we were expecting the mob to come howling along, a person [came with] a confidential message from a Catholic priest, that Gov. Seymour had taken responsibility of stopping the draft & the chief rioters were to be informed of this measure...."[27]

Whether or not George Templeton Strong was right in assuming that McCulloh and his Copperhead associates had taken part in the planning of the riots, there is no extant record of McCulloh's sentiments before he abandoned New York City for the Confederacy. By the time Professor McCulloh arrived in Richmond in early August 1864, the Confederate defeat at Gettysburg indicated that hope was fading at the highest levels of command. On August 8, General Robert E. Lee wrote to Jefferson Davis, offering his resignation: "The general remedy for the want of success in a military commander, is his removal.... I have been prompted by these reflections more than once since my return from Pennsylvania to propose to Your Excellency the propriety of selecting another commander for this army...."[28]

Others bravely put on hopeful faces in spite of their growing fears. Sally Brock Putnam, Richmond diarist, tells of "Richmond workshops turning out large supplies of valuable arms and weapons of warfare for battles sure to come, of our Nitre Bureau made effective in contributions of valuable ammunition ... while the idea of the final defeat of the cause for which we had fought had not yet possessed us, gloom pervaded our hearts."[29]

When McCulloh came to Richmond his reputation and secessionist sensibilities preceded him. He was armed with credentials, letters of praise and personal testimonials. John Botts Minor, a University of Virginia law professor and a pedigreed Virginia son, wrote to Confederate Secretary of War James A. Seddon. He hardly knew McCulloh and yet was willing to vouch for him:

> September 16, 1863
>
> I take the liberty of introducing to you acquaintance, the bearer of note, Professor Richard S. McCulloh, a gentleman of rare scientific attainments, whose wide spread reputation is probably not unknown to you ... His talents and attainments qualify him for extraordinary usefulness, and as my short personal acquaintance is sanctioned by the much more intimate knowledge of a common friend on whom I can rely, I take pleasure in making him known to you and commend him to your favorable considerations.[30]

Confederate Secretary of State Judah Benjamin, with an obvious prior personal knowledge of McCulloh, praised him in a letter to James A. Seddon:

September 25, 1863
Professor McCulloh, the bearer of this letter, is well known to me as a
gentleman of the highest character. He has abandoned a lucrative position at the North.... Because of his scientific attainments, I feel his
services will be of very great value in the development of our resources
in the ordnance or Nitre Bureau. Let me urge you to by all means to
use his services.[31]

His services now assured, McCulloh expressed concern that as a non-
commissioned private citizen involved in highly clandestine operations,
he would have no protection if captured. But according to McCulloh family chronicles, his descendants believed he was given a military commission and referred to him as "General" or "Colonel." After a careful search
of Confederate service records and other relevant materials in the National
Archives, no record was found to authenticate the family claim.

In spite of his status as a private citizen, McCulloh continued to
lobby Seddon for greater responsibility. He got it. On July, 16, 1864, he
was "detailed and authorized to proceed to join [go to] the army operating under General Early and to report to General Rains for assignment
to such duty as may be appropriate to his qualifications and for the benefit
of his services."[32]

While this was not an actual commission, it was surely a measure of
confidence, adventure and high risk. Apparently, it was not enough. In
a letter to Seddon, McCulloh requested (perhaps a ploy on his part) a
passport out of the Confederacy to conduct his wife and daughter to
Europe. McCulloh states he is without employment, and he might better serve the Confederacy while out of the country. There is no evidence
that he went abroad, but remarkably, on January 19, 1865, less than a
month after McCulloh wrote the letter, Secretary of War James A. Seddon gave him his much desired passport and much more: a license to
kill. Seddon wrote:

Sir, In granting you a passport to go beyond the limits of the Confederate States ... you are authorized, under an act to organize bodies for the
capture and destruction of the enemy's property by land and sea,
approved 17th February, 1864, to engage in the destruction of the
enemy's property on the high seas or the rivers, lakes and harbors in the
United States....[33]

Seddon then authorized McCulloh to organize a company "not to
exceed twenty in number" and asked him to forward a muster roll to the

War Department. Seddon emphasized McCulloh's services would be rendered without pay.[34]

To date, the aforementioned muster roll has not been located. However, among the papers of the Confederacy found after the fall of Richmond was a secret roster of Confederate operatives working directly for President Jefferson Davis and Judah Benjamin with the operatives' code names and cipher keys. The list included such clandestine luminaries as Jacob Thompson and Thomas Hines. McCulloh, whose code name was "Richard," was paired with former representative from Missouri to the Confederate Congress Thomas A. Harris. They shared in the development of chemical weapons and were given the common code name "Constantinople" by their handlers.[35]

Thomas A. Harris would factor prominently in the planning and execution of Professor McCulloh's chemical weapon plan proposed in the letter to Jefferson Davis from Williamson Simpson Oldham. He urged President Davis to consider McCulloh's perfected formula, which attests to the perceived need for a final chemical solution.

From all evidence, it appears that a weapon or weapons had indeed been perfected. In all probability, there may have been two formulas: one, a perfection of Greek fire and the other, a preparation that emitted a lethal gas. Dr. Linda McCurdy, the Director of Research Services in the Rare Book, Manuscript, and Special Collections Library at Duke University, speculated that one of McCulloh's preparations might have been a precursor to the "oxygen consuming gas: halon."[36]

Whatever the properties of the combustible (there is no extant formulaic record), the weapon would not be used. Less than a month after President Davis agreed to consider McCulloh's deadly preparation, Richmond fell. Recently discovered documents state that McCulloh and Thomas A. Harris fled through the Florida outback with five other associates of Davis' toward the coast and eventually to Cuba.

A Federal commander at Jacksonville, Florida, was told that some "suspicious characters" were escaping through the swamps in a tiny boat with a box of gold that they might have used to be taken to Tampa or Sarasota Bay. Supposedly they were with a Captain Johnson who knew how to navigate through the infested and secret byways of the Florida Keys.[37]

It was presumed that this group of fugitives contained high-ranking officers of the Confederacy. The steamy Florida outback was a mosquito and snake ridden tangle. With the Federal parties on their heels, the fugitives hid in stands of mangroves and traveled by boat when they could.

Farther down the coast near Cape Sable, Florida, Union Lieutenant J. J. Hollis of the 2nd Florida Cavalry and his guard had been alerted that the fugitives might be heading their way. By May 17, at 2:30 A.M., it was over. McCulloh, Harris and five others were discovered hiding in a cluster of mangroves and taken to Key West in chains. Because they were not high ranking Confederate officials, certainly not of the caliber and importance of Jefferson Davis and his cabinet, their capture was not widely publicized. That would change.

Testimony in the trial of the Lincoln conspirators had begun on May 12 in Washington, D.C. On May 18, Reverend W.H. Ryder of Chicago was called as a witness for the prosecution. Ryder revealed that during a trip to Richmond on the day of Lincoln's assassination, he visited the capitol and "found the archives of the so-called Confederate States scattered about the floor; and in common with others, took as many of these as I chose." Apparently, Reverend Ryder handed over papers "that seemed important or interesting" to the authorities.[38] The letter from Williamson Simpson Oldham naming Professor McCulloh as the progenitor of the weapon meant to spread "terror and consternation" was among the documents and produced as evidence in court. Following testimony concerning the verification of Oldham and President Davis' signature, prosecution witness Joshua T. Owen fully identified McCulloh: "I have known Professor McCullough [sic], I suppose, for twenty years; he was Professor of Chemistry at Princeton College.... He has, I believe, been at Richmond during the rebellion, the service of the Confederates ... he had attained some distinction as a chemist, perhaps more in that than in anything else."[39]

Richard Sears McCulloh was now much more than just a suspicious rebel. On May 14, George Templeton Strong's jubilant diary entry announced the capture of the Confederate President: "Jeff Davis has been bagged at Irwinsville, Georgia."[40]

On May 22, unaware of McCulloh's capture, but determined to imprison all of Davis' associates, Secretary of War Stanton issued a warrant for his arrest.

> Major General ORD, Richmond:
> Immediately upon receipt of this, arrest James A. Seddon, late rebel Secretary of War, and confine him securely in Libby Prison. Also arrest

and imprison Professor McCulloh, who is now, or recently was, in Richmond. Please spare no effort in the diligent execution of this order and regard it as strictly confidential.[41]

Details of McCulloh's flight and apprehension were emerging. J. J. Hollis reported the capture in a dispatch carried by the *New York Herald* on May 27, 1865:

> In obedience to orders received May 9, I proceeded to Cape Sable with a detachment of the Second Florida cavalry to intercept any persons who might be making their escape from the Confederacy. On the morning of the 17th at half past two a boat with sail set was seen near the shore. When the packet boat immediately pulled for it and upon challenging was answered, "a fishing boat." The corporal in charge of the packet boat ordered the crew to surrender, which they did without resistance, their revolvers having been wet by the surf and consequently useless. On being brought to camp, I examined every trunk, valise & finding considerable rebel money and a few papers which I still hold possession of. They appear to be an intelligent party of men and undoubtedly have held important positions in the Confederacy. They all acknowledge to have been in Richmond. The party consisted of seven white men and a colored servant.[42]

The *New York Tribune* of May 30, 1865, reported that on May 23, a "United States steamer, *Glaucus*, from Key West arrived in the tow of the steamer, *Magnolia*. The *Tribune* makes reference to the report of May 29th announcing the capture of "a mysterious party."[43]

The *New York Herald* fully identified the former Columbia professor: "Richard S. McCulloh is the professor in the rebel service, into whose hands was placed, according to evidence adduced upon the Washington trial, knowledge as to the composition of the combustible materials to be employed by secret agents in the incendiarism of New York and other Northern cities."[44]

Just a day before, on May 29, George Templeton Strong had not been so diplomatic: "A party of six or seven Rebel fugitives were captured at Cape Sable. That sneak Prof. McCulloh seems to have been among them."[45]

In a telegram to Stanton from Philadelphia on May 29, J.B. Harding, a former co-worker of McCulloh's in the Philadelphia mint, referred to the Lincoln conspirator's trial testimony:

Hon. E.M. Stanton

In the party of fugitives captured in a boat off the Florida coast on the seventeenth by L. Hollis is Professor McCulloh formerly melter and refiner in the Philadelphia Mint whose name appears in documents captured in Richmond as being in the 'poison and dagger service' of the Confederacy. In the trial of the assassins I saw the report of the evidence against him & take the liberty of calling your attention to his capture.[46]

Richard McCulloh and General Thomas A. Harris were transported in chains and under heavy guard from Key West, Florida, to the Washington Arsenal in Washington, D.C., the site of the final imprisonment and hanging of the Lincoln conspirators.

"During our charge of the prison," wrote Brevet Lieutenant Colonel Richard A. Watts, "we also received for safekeeping Burton Harrison, who had served as private secretary to President Davis.... Professor McCullough [*sic*] ... reputed to be a skilled chemist, and General Harris...." Watts also recalled that "after the execution and removal of the conspirators ... General Harris was taken to Fort McHenry." The Baltimore, Maryland, fort that inspired Francis Scott Key's "Star Spangled Banner" during the War of 1812 was by the time of the Civil War a military prison for captured Confederates. Thomas A. Harris remained there until his parole on August 8, 1865.[47]

Back in New York City on July 15, George Templeton Strong pondered McCulloh's likely fate: "Professor McCulloh in durance at Washington. If he is tried for arson, convicted and hanged, does etiquette require me as an acquaintance and a trustee of Columbia College to attend the execution?"[48]

Without the benefit of protection as an officer under military law, McCulloh was transferred to the Virginia State Penitentiary in Richmond. Designed by the renowned architect and engineer Benjamin Henry LaTrobe in the latter part of the eighteenth century, the forbidding stone structure was designed for solitary confinement and "surveillance as a means to reform prisoners through penitence and solitary reflection."[49] The prison "received no prisoners for petty offences, or for a term of confinement for less than one year ... those sent here are for rape, murder, and all the great social crimes, or political offenders of extraordinary interest."[50]

Richmond war clerk John B. Jones wrote of the starvation and disease endured by Richmond citizens at the end of the war, of how even

Sketches of cats drawn by Professor McCulloh while in solitary confinement in the Virginia State Penitentiary (courtesy of Richard and Anna McCulloch).

the cats were skeletal and roamed the filthy prisons in search of food. McCulloh family scrapbooks contain several sketches of cats that McCulloh made while in solitary confinement. His "visitors without a pass" were artfully drawn as they slipped through the prison bars or slept curled on the stone floors.

After eight long months, heeding the pleas of McCulloh's brother, Columbia College President Maclean, in a less-than-heartfelt letter dated December 12, 1865, to President Andrew Johnson, argued that McCulloh was probably reformed and not a danger to society. The government was not in the least convinced. McCulloh remained in solitary.

McCulloh's parole did not come for quite some time. Perhaps the authorities were waiting for proof that McCulloh's "weapon" had indeed been used and hoped for a confession. Perhaps the need to find enough evidence to justify the execution of President Davis was reason to keep an associate like McCulloh imprisoned.

The following is found with a contemporary sketch of the Virginia State Penitentiary in extant McCulloh papers: "In which prison I was held in close confinement for seven months from July 1865 to Febr. 1866 inclusive, and then put in Libby Prison."[51]

On March 25, McCulloh was released, paroled to New York, and

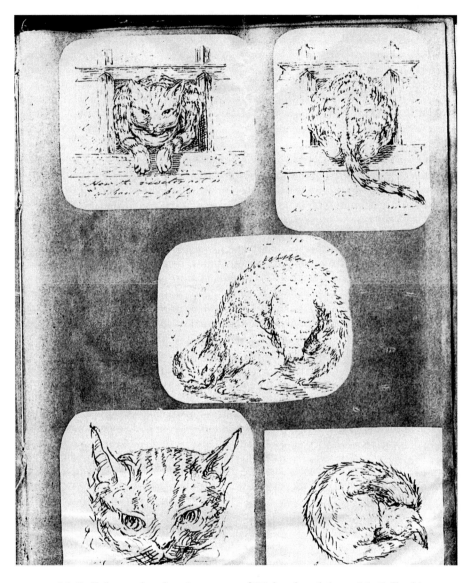

McCulloh cat sketches (courtesy of Richard and Anna McCulloch).

ordered to remain there. He did not stay for long. A powerful and sympathetic ally was waiting in the wings: Robert E. Lee. By now the president of Washington College (now Washington & Lee University in Lexington, Virginia), Lee invited McCulloh to apply for a post as professor of Natural Philosophy. On May 29, two months after McCulloh was paroled, Lee wrote, "your acceptance to the Professorship at Washington College, and the decision of the Board of Trustees, to which you have been unanimously elected ... gives me equal pleasure...."[52]

McCulloh's jubilation is evident in his response to Lee.

> Dear Sir,
> It was highly gratifying to me to learn that my election to a professor-

***Right*: Professor Richard Sears McCulloh in old age, circa 1890 (courtesy of Richard and Anna McCulloh). *Bottom*: McCulloh "Parole of honor" letter (courtesy of Richard and Anna McCulloch).**

ship in Washington College made with your full approbation and consent, without which I could not have felt free to accept or have desired the position. You will find me not only willing, but anxious to do all I can in aid of your plans and labors for the success of the institution and the course of education and learning in our dear Southern land, not less dear to us because of her sorrow and desolation....[53]

At Washington College, McCulloh dove back into academic sciences, lecturing on the *Mechanical Theory of Heat and the Steam Engine*, a volume later used at West Point.

In the fall of 1869, McCulloh went back to New York to attempt to raise funds for Washington College, a daring move considering his ignominious exit. While McCulloh was in New York, Lee sent him a letter containing an unusual and rare confidence:

Every brave people who considered their right attacked & their Constitutional liberties invaded, would have done as we did. Our conduct was not caused by any insurrectionary spirit nor can it be termed rebellion, for our construction of the Constitution under which we have lived & acted was the same from its adoption & for 80 years we had been taught & educated by the founders of the Republic and their written declarations which controlled our consciences and actions. The epithets that have been heaped upon us of "rebels" & "Traitors" have no just meaning, nor are they believed in by those who understand the subject, even by the North....[54]

Hudson Strode, biographer of Jefferson Davis, speculates that "perhaps Lee hoped his opinion might win those Northerners hesitating to make contributions."[55] Whether the Lee letter was a calculated attempt at Constitutional justification or a baring of the soul, the letter is remarkable. Apparently a warm relationship existed between the two men. Mrs. Robert E. Lee wrote on July 9: "My dear Col.: Will you come tomorrow Tuesday about a quarter past two to dine with us *en famille* in company with Col. Johnston & Family?"[56]

Lee died in 1870, but McCulloh remained at Washington College until 1877 when he transferred to the faculty of Louisiana State University, where he was given the chair of General and Agricultural Chemistry. McCulloh, by now a self-appointed colonel, was miserable there; age, temper, and growing paranoia and unhappiness pervaded his work.

By 1884, he was dropped from the faculty of Louisiana State because of unexplained personal difficulties. In a letter to his brother dated

Letter from Mrs. Robert E. Lee to Professor McCulloh (courtesy of Richard and Anna McCulloch).

November 29, 1885, McCulloh, the unreconstructed southerner, speaks of his life as being "nothing but bitter disappointment, in which there was nothing to envy.... The North had become to me as a foreign land.... I took pride in preparing a textbook for Columbia. It was my final adieu to the North." It was the gift of his broken sword to the victors from a vanquished rebel — his salutation and surrender, his 'moriturno te salutat.'"[57]

Despondent and ailing, Richard McCulloh visited his brother John at the Oldfields School in Glencoe, Maryland. Back among the high-blooded horses of childhood, McCulloh died on September 15, 1894. His war was over.

SEVEN

Aimed at the President's House

"In my opinion all means of destroying our brutal enemies are lawful and proper."
Major General Daniel Harvey Hill, CSA, 1862*

April 2, 1865, Confederate Thomas Cooper De Leon remembered, was "as bright a Sunday as had shown in Richmond all spring."[1] That morning, President Jefferson Davis attended St. Paul's Church alone, having sent his wife and small children out of the city to what he prayed would be safe haven ... somewhere. A sexton walked down the aisle and whispered to him. In a nearby pew, Constance Cary "plainly saw the sort of gray pallor that came upon his face as he read a scrap of paper thrust into this hand."[2]

The scrap of paper was a telegram from Robert E. Lee:

> His Excellency President Davis, Richmond, Va.:
> I think it is absolutely necessary that we should abandon our position to-night [sic]. I have given all the necessary orders on the subject to the troops, and the operation, though difficult, I hope will be performed successfully. I have directed General Stevens to send an officer to your Excellency to explain the routes to you by which the troops will be moved to Amelia Court House, and furnish you with a guide and any assistance that you may require for yourself.
> R.E. Lee[3]

President Davis relayed the agonizing news to his staff. "It is true! The enemy have broken through our lines...." Confederate war clerk John B. Jones, like many in Richmond, "broken in health and bankrupt

---

*William A. Tidwell, James O. Hall and David Winfred Gaddy. Come Retribution: The Secret Service and the Assassination of Lincoln (Jackson: University of Mississippi Press, 1988), p. 157.

in fortune," wrote, "General Lee has dispatched the secretary to have everything in readiness to evacuate the city tonight."[4]

Immediately, President Davis ordered the wholesale destruction of government papers and made ready to abandon the Confederate capitol. War Department documents and official dispatches were pitched into the street and set ablaze. Officials laden with gold and personal belongings surged toward the Danville Railroad depot. Within hours, the trains bulged with Confederate congressmen, high-ranking cabinet members, Torpedo Bureau operatives armed with ordnance and wealthy citizens desperate to escape. "Grim terror that spread in wild contagion," wrote Richmond diarist Sally Brock Putnam, "carried word of the evacuations from house to house."[5]

Fearing mob panic, looting, or worse, city council members ordered all liquor supplies destroyed, but not before Thomas Cooper De Leon saw that "...the whiskey ran in the gutters ankle deep: and there half-drunken women and children even, fought to dip up the coveted fluid in tin pans, buckets, or any vessel available."[6]

"After night-fall," Sally Putnam wrote, "Richmond was ruled by the mob."[7]

In the Danville train depot office, a fevered Jefferson Davis paced the floors awaiting a telegram he prayed would announce the resurrection of Robert E. Lee's shattered armies. His friends begged him to flee. "I am waiting for better news," he reportedly told them. Finally, at 11 P.M., Davis boarded the train for Danville, the last out of the city that night. By April 3, Richmond was burning.

Ignoring the possibility that selective warehouse fires could not be contained, city officials, abetted by "a reckless military order," caused the conflagrations. The roar of the flames was heard above the shouts of people pushing through the black smoke as embers jumped from roof to roof, igniting houses, outbuildings, anything in their path.[8]

"Some of the great flour mills have taken fire from the burning government warehouses and the flames are spreading through the lower part of the city," reported John B. Jones. "The street was filled with negro troops, cavalry and infantry, and were cheered by hundreds of Negroes at the corners."[9]

Into this chaos came hundreds of Northern soldiers. Brigadier General Edward Hastings Ripley of Vermont, the Union commander at the capture of Richmond, watched as "The Confederacy died like a wounded wolf, gnawing at its own body in insensate passion and fury."[10] The once proud capitol had perished by its own hand.

Those who remained braved the fires and gas fumes to forage for food. What little remained was unaffordable. Flour was $1500 a bushel. Bacon, if it could be found at all, was $90 a pound. Armed looters pillaged markets not yet destroyed by the fires. Others stuffed corncobs into their pockets or hunted for rats.

With great irony, not lost on white former slaveholding residents, Union Major General Godfrey Weitzel and his black troops helped douse the flames. "I wish this conflagration stopped, and this city saved," General Weitzel told General Ripley. "If it is in the bounds of human possibility."[11]

It was a Herculean task. Retreating Confederates had cut the fire hoses and disabled the engines. "Above all this scene of terror hung a black shroud of smoke," Sally Putnam wrote, "through which the sun shone with a lurid angry glare...."[12]

Constance Cary ventured out of her attic room. "We walked through the streets like lost spirits until dawn," she remembered.[13] And Sally Putnam knew that into every house "terror penetrated ... the grief was too deep, the agony too terrible, to find vent in the ordinary channels of distress."[14]

The next morning, as a "deathlike quiet pervaded the great and tumultuous city,"[15] Abraham Lincoln's party steamed down the James River on the *River Queen* to view the vanquished capitol first hand. Nearly seven feet tall in his black stovepipe hat, with his young son Tad, a band of black soldiers and plainclothes guards as escort, Lincoln drifted like a giant crane through the smoking streets. Except for the occasional crack of burning timber, Richmond was still.

Former landed gentry, many of whom were near starvation, watched from behind closed shutters as the Yankee president stopped to greet hundreds of former slaves who mobbed him, hungry to look, Sally Putnam observed, "to shake his hand, to hear the tones of his voice."[16]

A few hours later as a weary Lincoln rested inside the Confederate White House in Jefferson Davis' mahogany chair, a Confederate soldier walked through the descending dusk to warn the Northern authorities of a terrorist plot aimed at the President and the most prominent and beloved symbol in the Union.

Brigadier General Edward Hastings Ripley took a hard look at the soldier, deemed him "a more than usually intelligent and fine appearing man in uniform by the name of Snyder" and heard him out.[17]

The "unusually intelligent" man was William H. Snyder of Company E, 2nd Virginia Cavalry, on detached duty with the Torpedo Bureau.[18] With little hesitation and much assurance that his story was not an act of betrayal but a clearing of the conscience, Snyder talked.

Although details were vague, a project had been set in motion that was, according to Snyder, unstoppable. Within minutes, Ripley summoned his adjutant, Captain Rufus Putnam Staniels, and ordered him to take Snyder's statement — fast.

"He was particularly anxious to tell me that a party had just been dispatched from

Brigadier General Edward Hastings Ripley, Union commander at the capture and occupation of Richmond.

Rains' Torpedo Bureau, on a secret mission, which vaguely he understood was aimed at the head of the Yankee government," General Ripley recalled, "and he wished to put Mr. Lincoln on his guard and have impressed upon him that just at this moment he believed him to be in great danger of violence and he should take greater care of himself ... that the President of the United States was in great danger."[19]

While Snyder claimed to be ignorant of the details, historians James O. Hall, David W. Gaddy, William A. Tidwell, Edward Steers, Jr., and most recently, this author, have pieced the plot together.

Torpedo Bureau explosives expert Sergeant Thomas Francis Harney and his guide, Thomas Franklin Summers of Elijah White's 35th Virginia Cavalry, were on their way from Richmond to plant explosives under the Lincoln White House. Harney had been hand-picked for the job. He'd long been in the business of blowing things up.

The informant William H. Snyder was no ordinary Rebel. He too was a Torpedo Bureau operative, assigned to the secret Confederate organization that was responsible for many of the concussions that had obliterated Northern encampments, depots, ships and harbors throughout the war.

According to Snyder, he had been approached by Lieutenant Samuel Gooch Leitch, a young University of Virginia medical student and "former ordnance officer in Pickett's division" assigned by General Rains in 1864 service to the Torpedo Bureau.[20]

Leitch told Snyder he "was in the Secret Service of the Confederate States, he asked me if I did not want an appointment." When Snyder asked "many questions" about the nature of what the Secret Service was planning, Leitch wouldn't give specifics; rather he said the "Congress [Confederate] was then in secret session upon a Bill authorizing the organization of a Secret Bureau the object of which ... was the organization of a Corps for the purpose of carrying on a systematic crusade upon the enemy.... I was asked to suggest something the destruction of which would inflict [word illegible] upon the North," Snyder said "I was told I would be aided in anything I would suggest or undertake ... furnished with gold or silver and aided by the Confederate authorities.... When Richmond was abandoned I remained here and now place in the hands of the authorities through General Ripley this information with the belief that it will be the means of saving not only the lives of women and children and other noncombatants but a vast amount of public and private property as well."[21]

Leitch, then the acting head of the bureau in Rains' absence, again attempted to recruit Snyder again in late March of 1965:

> Dear Snyder,
> Old acquaintances should never be forgot — the Bill has passed organizing our corps. Should the present incumbent remain you had better [illegible] around for a commission. We can have some fun this summer.... A word to the wise.
>   S.G. Leitch[22]

If Leitch's mention of "fun this summer" and "the present incumbent" (clearly referring to Abraham Lincoln) was ever examined, it was never acted upon. On March 30, 1865, Leitch reported that the bureau had only "two operators present."[23]

One of them, Frank M. Blackwell, does not appear to have been sent on the bombing mission. The other remaining Torpedo Bureau operator was explosives wizard Thomas F. Harney.

Knowing the Torpedo Bureau had one last job to do, William Snyder told General Ripley about a "project" that would deal a final blow to the Union. When Ripley demanded to know more, Snyder clammed up. "The President of the United States was in great danger," was all he would say.[24]

Ripley sent an urgent message to Lincoln aboard his temporary residence, the flagship *Malvern*. Word came back quickly in Lincoln's own hand. He would see Ripley at nine A.M. sharp. "By dawn, I was promptly on hand, taking the Confederate soldier with me," Ripley wrote.[25] By now he was convinced Snyder was telling the truth.

Ripley boarded the Malvern and rushed to President Lincoln's side. Over the whoops of glee emanating from Lincoln's young son Tad as he scrambled over the furniture, Ripley read Snyder's statement aloud to Lincoln. With the face of "a man of sorrows and acquainted with grief," Lincoln brushed Snyder's warning aside, saying, "'I cannot bring myself to believe that any human being lives who would do me any harm.'"[26] With that, the interview ended. After Lincoln left for Washington, Ripley wrote, "I never saw him again."[27] His failure to convince Lincoln of the peril he faced haunted him. Years later, he still agonized: "I have so often thought of the web of fate I held in my impotent hands that morning … had I only been able to persuade the great president to let his friends protect him until the first rage of the enemy over defeat had expended itself."[28]

It seemed that Lincoln's death was imminent, but not at the hands of John Wilkes Booth. Plans to decapitate the entire government were at the ready.

Partial details of the plot were found in Lincoln assassination conspirator George Atzerodt's confession, which was discovered by historian Joan L. Chaconas "among the papers of William E. Doster, who had served as defense attorney for Lincoln Conspirator George Atzerodt."[29]

Just after his capture, Atzerodt related details of a "project" to "get the president certain." According to Atzerodt, John Wilkes Booth told him that a group of men he'd met with in New York were going to "mine the end of the President's house near the War Department." He added that "They knew an entrance to accomplish it through."[30]

The War Department was located on the southwest corner of Pennsylvania and 17th Street, a short walk down a tree-lined gravel path from the White House.

"To effect the demolition, an expert in the use of explosives was required," authors Hall, Tidwell and Gaddy have stated. "There was no such person in the Booth group. One would have to be found and brought in."[31]

Atzerodt added that the explosion would occur during a serenade (often an impromptu trumpet concert common at the time of war's end) for Lincoln. "Spoke about getting friends of the Presdt. [*sic*] to get up an entertainment & they would mix it in, have a serenade & thus get at the Presdt. [*sic*] and party," Atzerodt said, adding "these were understood to be projects."[32]

Lincoln was to arrive back in Washington from Richmond late on the afternoon of April 9. On April 10, Lincoln and his entire cabinet were in the White House for a meeting. According to a chronology of Lincoln's activities and whereabouts that day, "crowds serenaded the President through the day. At five P.M., a jumble of revelers and musicians assembled at the White House."[33] On cue, over the jubilation of the crowd, Thomas F. Harney and his accomplice or accomplices would place the bomb and detonate it with a timing device, a fuse or by simple ignition.

Diagrams of the Lincoln White House show the President's office next to the Cabinet room on the second floor. According to James O. Hall, a large explosive placed under the joists of the first floor in all probability would have caused the floor to collapse causing the unsupported second floor to fall as well, resulting in the ultimate demolition of the building.

With a man like Thomas F. Harney in charge, it was the perfect scheme. And if he or his operatives perished, in all probability they would have been viewed as martyrs to the lost cause.

In fact, Harney was often surrounded by men who would willingly trigger explosives, war-weary soldiers who perhaps might envision a heaven replete with grand mansions, happy slaves, beautiful belles and cotton as far as the eye could see. Far preferable to the reality of ruined homes, blackened crop fields, cities like Atlanta and Richmond turned into refugee camps and the humiliation of occupation, a long lost paradise might be sweeter by far.

But the man with the bomb remains an enigma. Study of his path from U.S. Army deserter, schoolteacher, confederate soldier, submarine battery engineer, torpedo planter and, finally, the head of the White

House demolition mission, has been riddled with twists, dead ends, victories and inconsistencies, not unlike the story of Missouri where some say the Civil War legitimately began, the state Thomas Harney called home.

Missouri, with all its improbable and conflicted aspects, was a killing field. Existing Balkanized sensibilities, pre-war guerrilla border raids from pro-slavery Bushwhackers and anti-slavery Kansas Jayhawkers created a war-within-a war well before 1861, the state was a boil of factionalism and slaughter.[34]

Governed by radical secessionist Claiborne Jackson, Missouri drafted its declaration of secession from the Union on October 31, 1861, in an "act declaring the political ties heretofore existing between the State of Missouri and the United States of America dissolved ... the government has wantonly violated the compact originally made ... by invading with hostile armies the soil of the state, attacking and making prisoners of the militia ... forcibly occupying the State capitol ... seizing and destroying private property, and murdering with fiendish malignity peaceable citizens, men women and children ... (Missouri) does again take its place as a free and independent republic...."

The State's freedom and independence did not occur until after anti-slavery Union General Nathaniel Lyon occupied the arsenal at St. Louis in an effort to keep Missouri in the Union. On May 10, 1861, Lyon imprisoned the Missouri Militia. As his troops "marched them through St. Louis," they were surrounded by pro-secessionists who allegedly threw rocks and yelled "Hurrah for Jeff Davis!" Lyon's men opened fire, killing 28 and wounding 75 civilians. The Camp Jackson massacre, as it came to be known, "galvanized the pro-secessionist Missouri Legislature."[35]

The secession act was passed. Missouri joined the Confederacy on November 2, 1861. So, apparently, did Thomas Harney. "Whether Missouri actually seceded or not depends on perspective," historians Deborah and George Rule wrote. "The state never fully left Union control, nor was it considered part of the Confederacy by the Union."[36]

According to Harney, he taught school in Harrisonville, Cass County, Missouri, when the war began. Formed in 1830 and settled by westward moving pioneers, Kentuckians, Indianans and Virginians, by 1861 Harrisonville had a population of 675 or 676 if schoolteacher Harney is to be included. Because no record has been found to verify his claim of residence in Harrisonville, it is possible that as a teacher or tutor he boarded with a family or relatives and was therefore an impermanent figure escaping the notice of census takers who often recorded residents based on incorrect or misunderstood information.

According to his service record, Harney enlisted at the age of 24 in the Missouri State Guard in 1861 when the governor was authorized to reform the old militia into a formidable fighting force. Serving as a Sergeant in Company C, 3rd Regiment Infantry, 8th Division, Harney was now part of a ragtag but ferocious band of 6,000 untrained soldiers led by Governor Claiborne Jackson and Colonel Sterling Price.

"In all their motley array," wrote Colonel Thomas L. Snead of the Missouri State Guard, "there was hardly a uniform to be seen.... There was nothing to distinguish their officers, even a general ... save a bit of red flannel, or a piece of cotton cloth.... But for all that they were the truest and best of soldiers.... Among them there was hardly a man who could not read or write ... and help her [the South] in her hour of great peril."[37]

Initially the State Guard's opposition was 1,000 German-Americans from St. Louis, commanded by General Franz Sigel at the Battle of Carthage, thought by some to be the first major land battle of the Civil War, on July 5, 1861, hours after President Lincoln declared war on the Confederate States of America. The battle was fought on the undulate prairie 12 miles north of St. Louis and eventually the Union forces were driven out of the city by the Guard. While the North proclaimed Victory, Sigel was not able to force the Guard from joining other troops moving north from Arkansas.

The Battle of Oak Hills or Wilson Creek followed on August 10, 1861. Thomas Harney was in the thick of it. While he left no record of his war experiences, many others did. Colonel Randolph Harrison Dyer, of the Missouri State Guard, wrote to his sister.

> On Saturday last we had one of the most terable [sic] battles that was ever fought on this continent, resulting in the defeat & route [sic] of the entire federal Army.... Such scampering of wagons & rushing to arms was never seen.... And notwithstanding the great advantage in the ground & of a sudden surprise, on the enemy's part, our men soon formed and commenced driving them back at every point ... not until after six hours hard fighting were they entirely routed.[38]

After the battle, the Guard was joined by Confederate forces from Texas, Arkansas and Louisiana in what was to become, in the words of the Missouri Division of the Sons of Confederate Veterans, a "federal humiliation."[39]

Harney's next battle at Dry Wood Creek, or Battle of the Mules as it is sometimes known, was just that. On September 2, 1861, in an effort to fully control Missouri, "Jayhawkers" commander U.S. Senator Colonel James M. Lane's "Red Legs" Kansas Cavalry pursued the Confederate forces. At Dry Wood Creek, the Confederates overpowered the Union Cavalry and captured their mules. Harney and the Guard headed toward Lexington in Lafayette County, Missouri.

The Guardsmen marched on Lexington. Home to three colleges on the "picturesque bluffs overlooking the broad Missouri River," the city was "also the center of wholesale and retail trade for a large section of western and southern Missouri."[40]

Apart from the fact that Lexington was a Confederate victory, hastily constructed breastwork made of hemp bales saved the day for Price's forces. "All Price's efforts, notwithstanding his overwhelming force, had failed to occupy the open space between the entrenchments and the river ... every time he repeated the attempt his troops were hurled back ... taking possession of some bales of hemp.... Price ordered them to be rolled into the river until they were saturated beyond any chance of fire.... He ordered a portion of his troops to roll them backwards, while others ... below the level of the moving parapet ... delivered their volleys as they went."[41]

On March 2, 1862, the battle of Elkhorn Tavern or Pea Ridge in northwest Arkansas cemented Union control of Missouri, but not before Daniel Martin, a Union man "borned in Arkansas," wrote a song about the fight: "I fled from those base rebels / Who fear not God or law ... I served four months at Rollie / Through sleet, snow and ice / And next received my orders: / Go meet old Sterling Price / That 'old secession' traitor / He didn't like the fun / He gathered up his rebel band / To Arkansas he run ... At a tavern called Elkhorn / They threw themselves around us / In the dark shade of night / And planted out their batteries / And waited till daylight."[42]

After Price was driven from the state having suffered the loss of 4,600 Confederate soldiers, the Confederate threat to Missouri was effectively over. When Harney and his fellow guardsmen could not stave off Northern invaders as they occupied Missouri, they scrambled to enlist in official Confederate regiments.

On May 1, 1862, Harney joined the 6th Missouri Infantry as a private and fought in the Battle of Iuka, Mississippi, on September 19, 1862, another Union victory. At the Battle of Corinth, Mississippi, on October 3, 1862, he was severely wounded in the arm and back by a minnie ball, a conically shaped bullet enlarged at the base by ridges. When fired from the "rifled musket, it allowed this bullet to be fired at a much faster speed.... The minnie ball would spiral through the air and upon contact could shatter the bone...."[43]

Unlike many in his regiment who died of wounds sustained by the new projectile, Harney survived. His regiment left him behind to recuperate in Abbeville, Mississippi, and he was captured a scant eight weeks later at College Hill, Mississippi, and was incarcerated in Gratiot Street Prison in St. Louis, Missouri. "Originally known as McDowell's Medical College, it was a strange-looking gray stone building that consisted of a three story octagonal tower and two wings."[44]

Operated by the Union army, Gratiot swarmed with spies, guerrillas, and Confederate prisoners of war. The prison sat in the middle of factional St. Louis, so escapees could find safe houses just blocks away. Prison records reveal that many of the most intrepid trans–Mississippi clandestine operatives, saboteurs and boat burners passed through Gratiot during the Civil War.[45]

Formerly a slave pen and auction house, Gratiot had the capacity to house two hundred prisoners. By the time Harney arrived, two thousand men were crammed body-to-body in unventilated chambers with one waste bucket to 50 men.

Upon his admission to Gratiot, in spite of the fact that prevarication might have gained him his freedom, on March 25, 1863, Harney stood proudly by his Confederate service record, stating that he was a Southern sympathizer and did not wish to have the authority of the United States government restored. He repeated that he was a schoolteacher before the war, owned one slave, had no wife or children and would not take the oath of allegiance.

Harney also informed the authorities that he was born in Blair County, Pennsylvania, and was currently a resident of Harrisonville in Cass County, Missouri, but historian James O. Hall, diligent genealogists and this author have turned up nothing to substantiate his statements. Either he slipped in unrecorded, an impermanent vapor leaving no trace of his origins, or he created a nom de guerre — an alias donned for his entire Confederate service.

Harney applied for and was granted "a few hours parole" to attend to "business in St. Louis."[46] He melted into the city. There is no record of just how long he remained "on business," but apparently his disloyal sympathies were no secret to the informants hired by the prison staff to prowl the city streets, listening for "secesh talkers."

A recently discovered arrest warrant dated February 24, 1863, reveals Harney's fate.

> Special order No. 19:
> Captain Peter Tallon, chief U.S. Police or any U.S. Police officer, will arrest Thomas F. Harney and commit him to the Gratiot Street prison, charged with being a Rebel soldier.[47]

It is possible that Harney was again released briefly when a small-pox epidemic swept through the airless prison. Fed little more than the meager rations of their charges, guards were dying at the rate of one a day — prisoners at the rate of six. Harney and others not infected were moved to a holding pen and prepared for exchange as "dead wagons" hauled away many of their unlucky comrades. Union Major General John A. Dix and Confederate Major General Daniel Harvey Hill agreed upon standards for prisoner exchange on July 22, 1862, according to historian and feature writer Daniel Moran: "Each rank structure would be permitted exchange for a service member of equal rank or a set number of privates and ordinary seamen based on the senior ranking service member to be exchanged."[48] A civilian for another civilian of equal standing would also be exchanged.

According to Harney, his exchange was delayed when he was ordered to appear as a witness in the court martial of Captain John Hogendobler, a prison guard. Apparently, Hogendobler had been charged with "conduct unbecoming" and "conduct prejudicial" when he "grossly insulted Mrs. Miriam Meredith," a Sister of Mercy, a "religious and loyal lady," who was distributing clothing to suffering and needy prisoners. He also allegedly told two guards to "shoot prisoners who were near the windows."[49]

Angered by the delay, Harney protested his lingering detention in Gratiot to Captain James A. Dwight, Provost Marshal General of the Department of the Missouri, on April 18, 1863:

> I am a resident of Cass County Mo and was captured at College Hill (Miss) on the 5th of Dec. 1862 from wounds received at the battle of Corinth and was paroled the same day. On the 29th of Dec. I received

a pass as a prisoner of war from Maj. Genl U.S. Grant to pass the United States military lines to my home in Cass County Mo. I returned home and remained there as a <u>loyal</u> <u>citizen</u> [Harney's underline] until February 26, 1863 when I presented myself to Capt Allen [illegible] expecting to be sent on exchange. I am now summoned as a witness … in a case "The United States versus Captain John Hogendobler," my name having been erased from off the exchange list two different times. As the court is indefinitely postponed, I wish to be [illegible] on parole to report myself in person or writing as often as you may deem necessary…. Under like circumstances, I know a parole would be granted to a Federal soldier by the Confederate authorities….[50]

On May 15, Harney was still in Gratiot. Again, he wrote to Captain Dwight, barely containing his outrage at his continued durance: "I could have been enjoying the blessings of home … my name having been placed on the exchange list and erased by your order two different times. If it is in violation of the rules to grant the above request, sooner than remain in prison all summer I will write to the War Dept for parole stating my reasons…."[51]

Rains' sketches of the sub-terra shell (land mine) invented by Brigadier General Gabriel James Rains, CSA (courtesy of the Museum of the Confederacy, Richmond, Virginia).

Whatever disinformation Harney might have fed to his interrogators, by June 2, 1863, he was sent to City Point, Virginia, Grant's headquarters on the James River to be exchanged. General Gabriel J. Rains of the Torpedo Bureau arrived on the same day. Rains needed men with war experience, brains and a fanatical devotion to the Confederacy to plant his prized land mines. It was promised that Rains would make such a man a sergeant in the Torpedo Bureau, pay him well, and if chosen, would serve the cause.

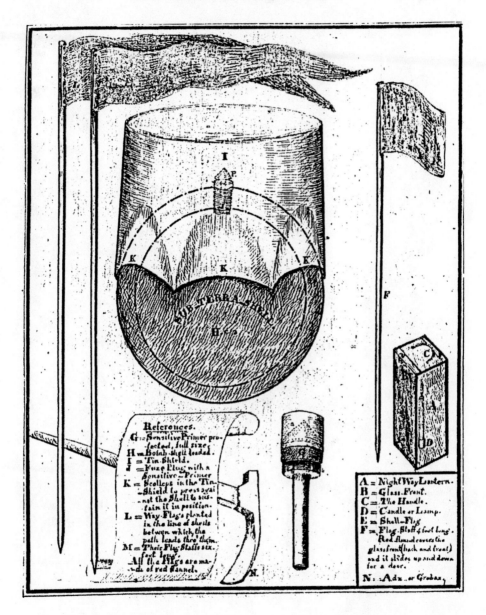

Another of Rains' sketches of sub-terra shell (courtesy of the Museum of the Confederacy, Richmond, Virginia).

Sergeant Thomas F. Harney, age 26, from the killing fields of Missouri, apparently met all of Rains' qualifications. One day later, he plunged into the belly of irregular warfare.

The first thing a trusted irregular must obtain is a horse — an unmarked animal that does not bear a Union or Confederate brand. In a time when free passage was anything but guaranteed, a plain clothes operative like Harney could slip by unnoticed in whatever disguise he chose to accomplish his explosives work.

Historian James O. Hall located a requisition signed by Rains to furnish Harney with a horse for temporary detached service with Rains' commanding officer General James Longstreet.[52]

Harney was placed in command of 40 men, grenade operators (possibly the more lethal the dart grenades invented by Rains), and land mine planters who swarmed behind Union lines leaving shattered civilians, soldiers, horses and equipment in their wake. Even Confederate General Longstreet questioned these tactics, "condemning this dastardly, immoral, if not illegal, method of waging war."[53]

Rains defended the actions of men like Harney in a terse memorandum to the Confederate War department with an endorsement from his immediate superior, crusty D.H. Hill, that "in my opinion all means of destroying our brutal enemies are lawful and proper."[54]

From January to February 1864, in a perilous effort to destroy the Confederacy's "brutal enemies," Harney was in Charleston, South Carolina, constructing torpedoes as well preparing and planting subma-

Brigadier General Gabriel James Rains, CSA, inventor of the land mine (courtesy of the Museum of the Confederacy, Richmond, Virginia).

rine batteries. General Gabriel Rains' "Torpedo Book" contains elaborate instructions for the construction of the Submarine mortar battery (non-electric variety) beginning with the procurement of "3 pine logs some 60 feet long ... at an angle of 45 degrees which must admit of an area 1 foot square ... to put submarine mortar shells upon." The logs would then be bolted and "affixed with 'light wood'" to serve as floaters. "A spike or pointed iron pin is to be driven into the small end of each beam ... through a hole in the center beam near the place of the shell," through which a chain would be passed and "fastened to the weight." A wire, "such as is used for telegraphs," would be threaded and fastened. Finally, the submarine mortar shell, hollowed and "one foot in diameter" was screwed on the float and placed in the hole before detonation.[55]

Special requisition for explosives expert Sergeant Thomas F. Harney signed by Brigadier General Gabriel James Rains (courtesy of James O. Hall and the National Archives).

It is doubtful that Harney placed electric (galvanized) batteries as Rains considered them inferior. Hunter Davidson, Rains' rival in the Navy Department, also engaged in making torpedoes. Davidson "specialized in electric control systems, whereas Rains preferred mechanical devices."[56]

By late February, Harney was dispatched to Mobile Bay, Alabama, listed in the Compiled Confederate Service Records in the National Archives as an operator (a torpedo planter). He was paid two dollars a day for his services with the possibility of extra pay commensurate to 10 percent of damages inflicted on Union ships. Most likely at the disposal of such an operator, according to historian Milton F. Perry, would have been "a manufactory, several rowboats, and various military units ... to protect them during an operation.... The boat crews ... wore dark clothing and caps when on duty ... oars were muffled with gunnysacks," he wrote. Smoking was, of course, prohibited and "side arms (revolvers and cutlasses) and ... sawed-off shotguns were carried by the crew" while officers would "look through spyglasses, look at the charts, figure moon and tide schedules...." The work was highly dangerous, especially for Harney, the "torpedo planter."[57]

Whatever his remuneration, Harney's assignment in Mobile is particularly significant. The lethal Confederate submarine, the CSS *Hunley*, had recently rolled off the dock. It is likely that Harney constructed or planted the torpedo that armed the sub, the "infernal machine," of the Confederacy.

He appears to have been present on February 16, 1864 when the tiny *Hunley* stole through the night and sent a torpedo into the side of the Union vessel the *Housatonic*. While the entire *Hunley* crew drowned just after this fourth and final mission, they managed to sink the *Housatonic*. It is tempting to imagine Thomas Harney, flushed with victory and pride at the sight of the great ship disappearing below the black water.

By the end of March 1865, Harney was summoned back to Richmond to continue his explosives work with the Torpedo Bureau. In spite of growing desperation within the Confederate ranks, much of the leadership in Richmond refused to believe all was lost. Planning was underway for an attack on a critically important target.

According to historians Hall, Gaddy and Tidwell, "A day or so before Richmond was evacuated on April 2 ... Harney left Richmond.... John Surratt was in the city with Confederate dispatch carrier Sarah Slater, who had come from Montreal with dispatches from Jacob Thompson and Edwin Gray Lee for Secretary of State Benjamin." "The connection seems obvious," they added, "the word was passed to activate the project mentioned by Atzerodt in his confession."[58]

Also present in Richmond was Harney's eventual handler, the infamous guerrilla chieftain Colonel John Singleton Mosby.

On approximately April 1 or 2, Harney boarded a train for Gordonsville, Virginia, a day's ride from Richmond. It is probable that Harney left Richmond with Torpedo Bureau fuses and timing devices. The actual explosives compound would be waiting for him in Washington.

The countdown had begun.

At Gordonsville, Harney met with the post commander, Major Cornelius Boyle, an important Confederate agent whose duties "involved the reception and forwarding of messages and agents between Richmond and Washington, D.C. When Harney reached Boyle's post, details of his arrival were relayed to Colonel John S. Mosby whose principal headquarters were near Upperville ... seventy-five miles north of Gordonsville."[59]

Step two of the mission was in play. Boyle furnished Harney with a horse (rare in those parts) and an all-important guide, someone familiar with every turn in the road, a fearless, intrepid irregular. A preponderance of evidence suggests that Thomas Franklin Summers, a former private in Colonel Elijah Viers White's 35th Virginia Cavalry, was the man chosen to lead Harney to the White House.

"Lige" White's cavalrymen were famous and fearsome, known for "Their wild charges, together with their blood chilling yells when they encountered any Union forces. I never called on White when he did not ride over everything in sight," stated General Wade Hampton.[60] "Commanche" Thomas F. Summers guided Harney to the headquarters of the guerrilla fighter and superstar hero of the behind-the-lines Confederacy, Colonel John Singleton Mosby.

Operating like latter-day commandos, Mosby's raiders had wreaked havoc on Northern troops throughout the Virginia countryside. Lauded in song and deed by the South, feared and hated in the North, Mosby was a legend. Able to slip through the trees, swooping down on his prey like a hawk, Mosby had a huge price on his head. He was a sharp stick in the eye of exhausted Northern generals who longed to see him hang. It was to this man that Harney was delivered on April 3 or 4, 1865.

In order to prepare a team to infiltrate Harney and Summers into Washington, Mosby hastily assembled company "H" on April 5 at North

Fork in Loudon County under the command of Captain George Baylor, "A youth who had already won distinction … in the Stonewall Brigade and the Twelfth Virginia Cavalry."[61]

With no clear purpose other than to effect the last mission of the war, the rest of the company were hand picked, battle hardened raiders from other Mosby units who were prepared to take Harney and Summers across the Potomac River at Upperville, Virginia, and wait while they slipped into Washington, met with agents who would supply them with the explosives and detonate them under the joists of the White House. Everything was so far going according to plan.

A portion of Company H left Upperville on Saturday, April 8, "marched to a small town called The Plains and dispersed with orders to meet the following morning." The stop was Arundel's Tavern, "on Ox Road, south of Burke Station on the Alexandria and Orange Railroad."[62]

Time was tight. The Federals were closing in.

"I received information … that a force of rebel cavalry was south of this post (Fairfax Station)," Colonel Charles Albright of the 202nd Regiment Pennsylvania Volunteers wrote. "I immediately ordered out all the cavalry I have under my command, and started in the direction indicated."[63]

The direction indicated was Burke Station. Company H, Harney and Summers moved at dawn. If pursued, they would fight. If captured, they had a cover. And if Harney and Summers couldn't make their escape, the men were told to say they planned to raid a mule train rumored to be at Burke Station. And Sergeant Harney, with timing devices and fuses on his person — what was he doing there? Sent to bring ordnance to Mosby, he would answer.

Enemy cavalry was spotted at Burke Station. Company H wheeled around and began firing as Harney and Summers escaped in the direction of Leesburg and the Potomac River. The 8th Illinois gave chase. The rest of Company H led the 8th Illinois back toward Fairfax Station, the planned feint abandoned.

To ensure a long skirmish, the men scattered in all directions, behind houses, trees and bushes as a detachment of Company K, 8th Illinois Cavalry "assaulted their rear, causing panic and confusion…."

The race was on. "At Arundel's [a tavern] I discovered them formed in line, as rapidly as I could, advanced, and opened fire," Colonel Charles Albright reported.[64]

Then, chaos. "Mohler's horse becoming exhausted, floundered in the mud near a sharp curve in the road," remembered Confederate James J. Williamson. As Mohler was dragged off his horse, the Cavalry opened fire. Raider Richard McVeigh was shot in the back. Edward Hefflebower and four others were trapped. While the remaining Raiders escaped, smashing men of the 8th Illinois with rocks, rifle butts, anything at hand, Harney and Summers reached the Potomac.

"I have just come into camp from a fight with a battalion of Mosby's men, under command of Captain Baylor," Charles Albright wrote. "I whipped him like thunder, captured a number of horses and some provisions. Had a few men wounded and a half dozen horses killed...."[65]

It was not over. A scouting party of the 8th Illinois had been dispatched to Loudon County on April 8 "for the purpose of scouring Loudon Valley in search of Mosby's command."[66]

The sight of two men scrambling through the brush at the river's edge must have seemed highly suspicious. "The scout under Colonel Clendenin, 8th Illinois Cavalry, has just returned. Captured two rebels..." Colonel William Gamble, Brigade commander reported on April 10.[67]

The "two rebels" Harney and Summers were first taken to the Fairfax Court House to be registered and sent on to the Alexandria, Virginia Slave Pen Guard House and finally to the Alexandria jail where they remained until April 12. Harney was now in the keep of the provost Marshal General of the defenses South of the Potomac at Alexandria.[68]

In an attempt to foil his captors, Harney gave his name as F.T. "Hearney." A hasty scrawl next to his name on the roster of prisoners points to the probable coercion used on Harney.

Whether he gave his true name or an alias in the heat of capture, Harney is listed as a "member of the Engineer (Torpedo) Bureau, Department of Richmond, found with ordnance," not as the simple infantryman he had once been.[69]

On April 12, Harney was moved to the Old Capitol Prison, a tumbledown brick building with "decayed walls, broken partitions ... creaking doors and staircases" at the corner of 1st and A streets N.E. in Washington.[70]

A record of Harney's transfer from Alexandria attests that Harney and Summers were captured separately.

Alexandria City Jail, Alexandria, Virginia. Thomas F. Harney was briefly held here after his capture (used with permission of Alexandria Library, Special Collections).

> Colonel (Ingraham)
> I have the honor to forward you under guard the following named prisoners Viz.
> D.G. Mohler
> Edwd. S. Hefflybower (actually Hefflebower)
> Samual Rogers
> M.W. Palmer
> Franklin Somers
> F.T. Hearney
> The first four men were captured by Col. Albright on the 10th inst...
> The last two named (Harney and Summers) were captured by a Scouting party of the 8th Illinois Cavalry.
> HH. Wells[71]

On his way to the Old Capitol Prison, Harney would likely have caught a glimpse of the White House. Perhaps he might have seen the mansion undisturbed, a profusion of April flowers covering the grounds.

With Harney's mission in ruins, it is likely that John Wilkes Booth decided to finish the job, but Booth was not an explosives man. His action team was ordered to decapitate the government. Lincoln died three days later in Ford's Theatre — shot in the head. Secretary of State William A. Seward barely survived a stabbing by conspirator Lewis Thornton Powell. Vice President Johnson, another intended target, was spared when George Atzerodt lost all nerve and wandered in a drunken haze through the streets of Washington.

John Wilkes Booth escaped into the southern Maryland countryside, ultimately aided in flight by Mosby men, a "leave behind" force ordered to abet Booth's escape after the assassination.

The city of Washington was grieving. Booth was at large, and the hunt for any accomplices was on. Secretary of War Edwin M. Stanton ordered "All persons harboring or aiding their concealment or escape will be treated as accomplices in the murder of the president and shall be subject to trial before a military commission, and the punishment of death."[72]

A massive dragnet was underway. Lincoln assassination conspirators were being rounded up and thrown incommunicado into the bowels of the ironclad USS *Saugus*. Leaders of the Confederacy, particularly Jefferson Davis and Judah P. Benjamin and Jacob Thompson, were blamed for complicity in the assassination. Thomas F. Harney remained in prison.

While the true purpose of Harney's mission remained unknown to his captors, they did not want a Torpedo Bureau man sitting in a cell in Washington in a prison that grew more crowded by the hour with men and women suspected of secessionist sensibilities.

On May 1, 1865, Harney was sent North to Elmira Prison in upstate New York just as the trial of the Lincoln's conspirators was beginning. Known to its luckless inmates as "Hellmira," "Elmira was nearer Hades than I thought any place could be," wrote G.T. Taylor, Company C, 1st Alabama Battalion of Heavy Artillery.[73]

Considered one of the most brutal Civil War concentration camps, its equal being Georgia's Andersonville Prison, by 1865 the death rate in this prison termed a "portal to hell" by historian Lonnie Speer averaged nine men a day. "I have seen a mob of hungry rebs besiege the bone cart," admitted one prisoner, "and beg from the driver fragments on which an August sun had been burning for several days."[74]

Harney remained at Elmira until July 7, 1865, one of the last batches of Confederates to be paroled. The last official mention of Harney, a record of release from Elmira, is perhaps the most provocative. "Place of residence: Leesburg Virginia. Complexion: Fair. Hair: dark, Eyes: Gray. Height: 5'9". Desires to go to his home at New Orleans, La."

On July 7, 1865, four of the Lincoln conspirators were hanged in a side yard of the Washington arsenal. That same day, Thomas F. Harney took the Oath of Allegiance to the United States and walked through the gates of Elmira Prison a free man.

Addendum

This author has recently found evidence to suggest that a man named Thomas F. Harney of Waterford County, Ireland, enlisted in the 2nd U.S. Infantry in May 1859 and deserted on November 11, 1860. The description matches that of the Missouri Confederate Thomas F. Harney except for the color of the hair.

EIGHT

"Again a part of the United States"

After his official pardon, John William Headley, implicated in the plot to burn New York City, lived quietly in Kentucky and Evansville, Indiana, before coming home to Kentucky in the late 1880s. He served as Secretary of State of Kentucky from September 1, 1891, to January 1, 1896. At the age of 60, he began to write his memoirs, *Confederate Operations in Canada and New York*. In winter 2002, this author located his gravesite. He died in Los Angeles at the age of 89 on November 6, 1930. He is buried in the Inglewood Park Cemetery.

Robert M. Martin's post-war years were spent in the tobacco industry working as a broker, warehouse supervisor and inspector. The commander of the New York arson project moved from Indiana to New York to Louisville, and finally back to New York. He died in the city he nearly immolated on January 9, 1900.

On February 11, 1878, Luke Pryor Blackburn announced his candidacy for governor of Kentucky, calling it "the most important event of my life" and an "opportunity to appeal to the people of my native state to expunge from my name that obliquy [*sic*] which the venal press and people of the North put on it at a time when no friend could defend me unless at the peril of his life and liberty."[1]

Blackburn's opponents, who told reporters that "a fiend and mass murderer" must not be allowed to govern the state, greeted the news with consternation. But the majority of Kentuckians didn't see it that way: Some approved of what the doctor had done during the war. After all, he had trumped "Bronze John." Others didn't care about what had happened 14 years earlier.

On September 2, 1879, a hot late summer day, Luke Pryor Blackburn was inaugurated as Governor of Kentucky and remained a popular figure in the state long afterward. He caused some controversy when he initiated widespread state prison reform. Blackburn died on September 14, 1887, in Louisville. Etched on his tombstone in the Frankfort Cemetery are the words "The Good Samaritan."

Colonel Jacob Thompson, head of the Confederate apparatus in Canada, fled to England after managing to secrete millions of dollars. After the trial of the Lincoln assassination conspirators, he was accused of masterminding the plots to burn cities and spread pestilence as well as complicity in Lincoln's murder. He denied it all. In 1868, he returned to the United States with a great deal of money harvested from Confederate funds. He died in Memphis, Tennessee, in 1885.

Edwin Gray Lee, Thompson's ailing young replacement who was charged with the handling of Lincoln conspirator John Surratt while a fugitive in Canada, died in his sleep of irreversible lung disease at the age of 33 on August 24, 1869. His second cousin, General Robert E. Lee, lauded him thusly: "I am truly sorry to hear of Edwin Lee's death. He was a true man, and, if health had permitted, would have been an ornament as well as a benefit to his race. He certainly was a great credit to the name...."[2]

Richard Sears McCulloh's chemical formula meant to bring "terror and consternation" heralded a descent into a different kind of warfare. Lethal gases and incendiaries of every variety have become commonplace since World War I.

McCulloh's cohort, Thomas A. Harris, "never surrendered. And up to the day of his death did not take an oath of allegiance." After the war he fled to Honduras and the Yucatan, "where he remained for about a year." He returned to the United States and settled in New Orleans where he became the founding editor of the *Times-Democrat.* Later, in Kentucky, he was Assistant Secretary of State under Governor Luke Blackburn. He died at his home, Locust Lodge, in Louisville on April 9, 1895.[3]

The land mine, the brain child of Brigadier General Gabriel Rains, remains a clear and present danger. Rains fled from Richmond to Georgia and moved to Charleston where he served in the U.S. Army's Quartermaster Department from 1877 to 1880. He died in Aiken, South Carolina, on August 6, 1881, at the age of 78.

The mysterious bomber Thomas F. Harney's intent was clear: the destruction of a beloved American landmark. It is likely that he changed his name and melted back into polite society.

Felix Grundy Stidger, the spy who brought about the fall of the Sons of Liberty, ran for his life to the end of his life. Of some consolation perhaps is a newly discovered record of a Secret Service payment to Stidger for his service to the United States of $10,000.[4] On December 23, 1903, an infirm, and fearful, Felix Grundy Stidger wrote to Francis M. Van Pelt in Anderson, Indiana, explaining the impossibility of travel outside his home in Chicago.

Felix Grundy Stidger, September 1903 (courtesy Nancy Clayton).

> I write to you under the name of M.S. Lawrence, as I have to, even to this day, be very careful to not unnecessarily expose myself.... I also have to this day a great many enemies in Indiana; but am thankful to be able to truthfully say that I am not afraid of the whole pack of them by daylight, but from assassination in the dark no man can protect himself ... I have had the experience of being followed by assassins paid by leaders of [the] Order of the Sons of Liberty for years to secretly assassinate me....[5]

It seemed that Stidger "was publishing a history of his experience" with the "damnable, treasonable organization the Sons of Liberty" and was trying to round up endorsements of old comrades to aid in the promotion of his book. "I was 67 years old the 5th day of last August," he wrote. "I shall probably never be able to visit your town...."[6]

A few years later, showing obvious confusion, Stidger again wrote to Van Pelt: "In 1864, coming to my mother's home at Taylorsville, Kentucky, where my mother died ... and I soon after being forced to leave my home, to which home I cannot I cannot [Stidger's repetition] return to this day under penalty of immediate death where I should be recognized even now...." Stidger died less than two months later on May 11, 1908.[7]

His obituary in the *Chicago Sun Times* refers to him as "the treason

Chicago, December 23rd, 1903.

F. M. VanPelt,
   Anderson, Ind.
Dear Comrade and Friend :
   Your very welcome and highly appreciated letter of 19th inst. just received, it being the first time I have been down town this week. I wrote you under the name of M. Sp Lawrence, as I have to, even to this day, be very careful to not unnecessarily expose myself.
   I am the original and only Felix G. Stidger, and remember well your visit to Taylorsville in the first part of April, 1864, and of Harry Whiteside, formerly John A. Murrell, being the pilot to Taylorsville, and of my piloting your command to the residence of Elijah Hughes, on Simpsons Creek, about five miles from Taylorsville, where you captured George Wells.
   My Mother had died but a few days before, and I left Taylorsville a few days after you was there, and have not been there since, and it would cost me my life to go there today. I also have to this day a great many enemies in Indiana; but am thankful to be able to truthfully say that I am not afraid of the whole pack of them in daylight, but from assassination in the dark no man can protect himself, and I have had the experience of being followed by assassins paid by leaders of Order of Sons of Liberty for years to secretly assassinate me, but I am still here and they are near all dead.
   The meetings you speak of in Indianapolis I do not remember, but know from your statement that they occurred.
   I had a good friend in the army; Captain VanPelt, commanding the 1st Michigan Battery, 1st Division, 14th Arcy Corps, Department of the Cumberland. He was killed at Chickamauga. I was not Provost Marshal at Taylorsville.
   I am publishing a History of my experiences with the damnable treasonable organization, the Sons of Liberty. It will be a book of 276 pages, and will a contain the only full expose of the grips, signs, and pass-words of that Order ever published. It will be issued in the first part of the next year.
   I was at one time a member of the G. A. R., but sickness compelled me to let my dues lapse, and I was dropped from the rolls. I was 67 years old the 5th day of last August. I shall probably never be able to visit your town, but shall at all times be glad to hear from you, and hope that I may some time meet you.
                       Fraternally yours, *Felix G. Stidger*
                       559 Orleans Street.

Felix Stidger letter from December 23, 1903 (from *The Knights of the Golden Circle, Treason History, Order of the Sons of Libery*, courtesy of Nancy Clayton).

plot exposer ... if he had passed away forty-five years ago, General Grant might have taken two more summers to have gotten to Richmond."[8]

On May 31, 2002, after years of searching, this author discovered the gravesite and headstone of Felix Stidger in Oak Woods Cemetery on Chicago's South Side. The letters, wrote *Chicago Sun Times* reporter Andrew Herrmann, are "worn almost invisible by nearly a century of Chicago wind and rain and snow."[9]

This author laid a wreath and read a eulogy. A snippet of poet Thomas Gray's "Elegy Written in a Country Churchyard," one of President Lincoln's favorites, was read aloud: "Some heart once pregnant with celestial fire ... hands that the rod of empire might have swayed, may be laid in this neglected spot...."

Appendix A

Coda

"How will the ministers conduct service under the new order of things?" many Richmond churchgoers wondered soon after their city had been occupied. U.S. Army Brigadier General Edward Hastings Ripley convened a meeting of Confederate clergy at his headquarters, noting, "The rectors of the Episcopal churches took the ground that as their form of prayer, established by the church of the South, required prayer for President Davis, no power could change it except that which created it."[1]

When confronted by Episcopal Rector Reverend Dr. Minnegrode, Ripley ended the discussion. "You forget sir," Ripley said, "that Richmond is again a part of the United States and under martial law. The services will be conducted with regard to loyalty to the United States."[2]

Thus liberated from the holy dictates on behalf of a leader in exile, all Confederates were expected to obey a new national order and rejoin the United States. Ripley, his career somewhat enhanced by war, predicted a unity of spirit and an ongoing state of forgiveness.

By the end of May 1865, having dubbed himself "the Duke of Richmond,"[3] General Ripley was ready to leave the broken Confederate capitol and go home to Vermont. He assured his mother that the Fourth of July would once again become a cause for national celebration and remembrance.

"Those who argue henceforth that the Fourth of July will be dull and stupid are wrong," he wrote. "Salutes to our flag will stir the blood of thousands of men ... and it will thrill through them like wine to a thirsty man."[4]

APPENDIX B

Arc of a Bomber: The Life and Death of William Stephen Deupree

It is always fortunate to obtain official records and family documents that reveal the secret and highly dangerous work of a Torpedo Bureau operative. The life and death of Virginia native William Stephen Deupree, a successful slave dealer and auctioneer turned Confederate soldier and operative, is here chronicled. Capitalization, emphases and punctuation are reproduced directly from the transcribed materials in the author's possession as well as official dispatches from the OR.

Deupree was born October 27, 1823, in Lunenburg County or Charlotte County, Virginia. His family established residence in Missouri, but Deupree remained in Virginia buying and selling land. He married Sarah Helen Emeline Williams in 1846, and finally became a County Court Justice of Lunenburg from 1852–1854. In 1859, he moved to Richmond, Virginia, and was soon "engaged in the slave auction business."[1]

On August 11, 1859, William Stephen Deupree wrote to his brother James R. Deupree after he had returned from a trip to visit the rest of the family in Missouri. The letter is notable for its description of the ease, optimism and good fortune of William Stephen Deupree just before the Civil War.

My dear brother:
This will inform you that we arrived home Monday night the 8th all safe and sound. We took boat to St. Louis (J.H. Dickey) for Memphis. We were late getting off and lay over at Cairo (where we took on heavy freight) about 10 hours; consequently we did not reach Memphis until Saturday morning about 1 0'clock just in time for the cars…. The rains have been general as far as I could ascertain until after we reached

Christiansburg in Va. The corn crop is good. Cotton bids fair to make a good yield so far, though it is too soon to decide. I find considerable advance in Negroes since leaving here in June, though I suppose I shall have to trade some at least. The weather has been warm but is quite pleasant now....[2]

A little less than a year later, William Stephen Deupree was an established slave dealer. A framed advertisement from the *Richmond Whig & Democrat* read as follows:

> Richmond, Virginia. Tuesday, July 24, 1860
> Auction and Commission House
> Odd Fellow's Hall
> Corner Franklin and Mayo Streets
> We have this day formed a partnership under the style and firm of DAVIS, DEUPREE & CO.
> For the purpose of selling NEGROES at public and private sale on commission. From our long experience in the trade, and by prompt attention to business, we hope to obtain the highest market price for all Negroes entrusted to us. We will make liberal cash advances on Negroes intended for our sales.
>   R.H. DAVIS
>   WM. S. DEUPREE
>   S.R. FONDREN
>   Rufus G. Maddux, Clerk
>   Richmond, June 4, 1860

National Archives records (card #50920647) indicates that Deupree joined the home guard as a private in Company B, 1st Battalion of Cavalry, Local Defense, "and on 11 March, 1864, he was paid $15.00 for supplying himself with one bay mare and $1.75 for equipment. This battalion was organized in July and August 1863 and was known as Browne's Reconnaissance Cavalry Corps and Browne's Battalion Cavalry, Local Defense. Also on card #51873047, he appears in Capt. Zach [*sic*] McDaniel's Company of Secret Service, residence Richmond subject to orders from Richmond; served seven months."[3]

Zedekiah McDaniel of Kentucky was a developer of the "horological" or time bomb. Prominent among acts of "destructionists" like McDaniel was the use of a clockwork bomb (torpedo) against the ordnance stores at Lieutenant General Ulysses S. Grant's City Point headquarters on August 9, 1864, an event that killed 58 people. Grant's on the spot dispatch to Major General Henry Halleck follows:

CITY POINT, VA, August 9, 1864 — 11:45 A.M.
Five minutes ago an ordnance boat exploded, carrying lumber, grape,
canister and all kinds of shots over this point. Every part of the yard
used as my headquarters is filled with splinters and fragments of shell. I
do not know yet what the casualties are beyond my own headquarters.... The damage at the wharf must be considerable both in life and
property. As soon as the smoke clears away I will ascertain and telegraph you....[4]

The explosion was at first deemed an accident, but General Halleck
informed Secretary of War Stanton that the explosion at City Point was
an act of sabotage.

I have just received the original official report of John Maxwell, of the
rebel secret service, of the blowing up of the ordnance stores at City
Point last year. It appears from this report that the explosion was caused
by a horological torpedo placed on the barge by John Maxwell and R.K.
Dillard, acting under the direction of Brig. Gen. G.J. Rains and Capt. Z.
McDaniel. I have ordered the arrest of these persons if they can be found.[5]

Captain Zedekiah McDaniel's operative William Stephen Deupree
was killed while planting a sub-terra shell (land mine) along the James
River on November 5, 1864, for the Torpedo Bureau.
Richmond Confederate soldier William L. Salmon described the
accident to Deupree's brother James:

I shall now endeavor to give you the particulars in regard to our dear
brother Stephen. He was a member of a Torpedo Company stationed in
Richmond and was engaged in planting 24 pound shells in front of our
works about eight miles below the city near Chaffins Bluff. In stooping
to place the shell in the hole just dug he lost his balance and fell over
upon it his right hand coming down on the spring which exploded the
shell killing him instantly. He was horribly mutilated having his right
hand and arm torn nearly off. One piece of shell passed through his
neck, one through his right eye and another lacerated his side dread-
fully. His face was so much disfigured that we could hardly recognize
him. His remains were decently interred in Hollywood Cemetery in his
lot. A great many friends attended the funeral....[6]

The "fellow secret service soldiers" in his company honored Deupree
at a meeting of Company E, 19th Virginia Battalion on November 10,
1864. "Capt. G.G. Savage; being called to the chair and J.A. Fisher;
appointed secretary, the following unanimously adopted":

1. RESOLVED, that in the death of WILLIAM S. DEUPREE, this company has lost a true and noble-hearted friend.
2. RESOLVED, that, after an intimate acquaintance of seven months with the deceased, receiving the hospitalities of his home and his uniform generous treatment in our camp, we are enabled, individually, and as a company to judge his noble traits of character; and which by these resolutions, to express for the deceased our high appreciation of his kindness to us while living, and tender to his family and friends the assurance that his memory is enshrined in our hearts; and wherever we may go, or whatever may be our fate, we will carry with us a grateful remembrance of his name and deeds.
3. RESOLVED, that as a member of the secret service of the Government he was esteemed a true and faithful soldier; and his sudden death, in the discharge of perilous duties, has brought to us, no less than to his older and more intimate friends, a severe and affecting grief.
4. RESOLVED, that we tender to his family, individually our condolences in this, the saddest of earthly afflictions, and give them the assurance of our protection while encamped near their home, and the remembrance of them as the kindest of friends when we leave.
5. RESOLVED, that a copy of these resolutions be published in the DISPATCH and furnished to the family of the deceased.
  Captain George G. Savage, Chairman
  James A. Fisher, Secretary
Camp near Richmond, Va., November 10th, 1864.[7]

On November 18, 1864, Torpedo Bureau head Brigadier General Gabriel J. Rains detailed the use of sub-terra shells (land mines) in a dispatch to Secretary of War James A. Seddon. Rains also includes a personal tribute to his valued operative, William Stephen Deupree.

SIR: I have the honor to state that notwithstanding the vigilance of the enemy, we have managed, from time to time, to transfer to their rear torpedoes; but many abortive attempts thus to destroy their shipping before I came here — but one success, I believe in the James River — have rendered them so watchful that I almost despair of accomplishing anything that way now, with the obstructions in the river and guards to their vessels. It has had one good effect, however, in causing the enemy to watch the river-banks with thousands of their soldiers, who might otherwise be employed against us. We have relied somewhat necessarily on the "Singer torpedoes," which were located at spots visited by the boats of the enemy, but, as before reported to the engineer bureau, with no adequate results, leading to a doubt of their efficiency in salt water where barnacles and young oysters abound. Our operations have been mainly directed to the James, Pamunkey, and Chickahominy Rivers, and some attempts made in Appomattox with torpedoes. When I left

Richmond for Wilmington, in the fall of 1862, we commenced planting submarine mortar batteries in the James, and it is much to be regretted that the officer who relieved me in the submarine defense did not continue their use, as these, the enemy report, being of a nature they could not remove, kept them out of Charleston harbor. Our efforts for the defense of this place have been directed lately to planting subterra shells between our lines of abatis at our works commanded by General Barton. We have planted at this date 1, 298 subterra shells so protected by tin covers inverted over them as thoroughly to shield them from the effects of rain and increase the area of the primer, and might thus be put at the bottom of the river without deteriorating their efficacy. For the protection of our own men, immediately in rear of each shell, at a distance of three feet, is planted a small red flag on a staff three feet long to indicate where it is, which is to be removed at night-fall or if the enemy approach, to be replaced as soon thereafter as necessary. There are pathways made for egress and ingress of our soldiers through these flags and shells indicated by longer streamers, and is intended to be surmounted at night by lanterns with lamp or candle having three darkened sides, and one glass covered with red flannel, as soon as they can be made; the pathway between two of these being safe at night, and the light easily extinguished at any moment. These shells now seem to be popular with our officers and are being planted as fast as our limited means will permit, say about 100 per diem. From reports of deserters they are rapidly demoralizing the enemy. Unfortunately in planting one of these shells a few days since one of our best men thus employed, WILLIAM S. DEUPREE, accidentally fell upon one and was immediately killed in full sight of the foe, who, hearing the explosion, was attracted to the spot, observing the effects and what was doing....[8]

Deupree's family memorabilia contain an obituary. The tribute appears to have been written by Deupree's partner in the slave auction business, S.R. Fondren.

To the memory of William S. Deupree.
The death of William S. Deupree, late of the county of Henrico, has occasioned his friends deep distress — and the writer, who knew him long and intimately, admired his manly virtues and enjoyed his friendship — to desire to bear, in a few words, his feeble testimony to the high qualities which adorned the character of the deceased. He was born in the county of Charlotte, in this State, and fell, in his forty-second year, on our lines below this city, in the discharge of his high. Patriotic duty. He possessed no ordinary intellect. He was a man of great integrity of purpose and energy of character. He possessed an amiable and cheerful disposition and the finest sensibilities. His deportment was gentle and his manners engaging. Few possessed greater philosophy, and none faced danger with greater intrepidity. He was ever ready to respond to appeals

for public or private charities. In all the relations of life his example is worthy of the highest commendation. As a husband and father, he was affectionate and kind; as a master, indulgent; as a friend, constant and true. He has left a widow and three children to mourn his death. May God, in his providence, so order their great affliction as to rebound their good.[9]

Deupree's wife Sarah wrote to her brother on May 30, 1865. The letter is here reproduced in part:

"I am in so much troubles I hardly know how to write or what to say. My dear husband was killed on the 5 of November by the explosion of a Torpedo. He belonged to that danjerious [*sic*] part of the army. I was very much opposed to his joining that Corps. I thought it must be so very danjerious [*sic*] he was planting them down on James River. He left home very early Sunday the morning he was killed, left about daylight. He came to the bedside and bid me farewell. Oh little did I think it would be our last interview, no, no it was the least of my thoughts."

William Stephen Deupree's estate was unsettled. Debts abounded. "I don't know what I shall do," Sarah Deupree wrote, "for everything we had was in Negroes and Confederate money except the land. I don't know what his creditors will do for the land will not bring enough to pay them all."

"For many years," the Deupree chronicles state, "Sarah Deupree had to make it on her own; she took in boarders."[10]

Chapter Notes

Chapter One

1. Walt Whitman, *Leaves of Grass* (Philadelphia: David McKay, 1900).
2. Muriel Rukeyser, *The Soul and Body of John Brown. The Columbia Book of Civil War Poetry* (New York: Columbia University Press, 1994), p. 123.
3. Ralph Selph Henry, *The Story of the Confederacy* (Old Saybrook, CT: Konecky & Konecky, 1931), p. 11.
4. Emory M. Thomas, *Robert E. Lee* (New York and London: W.W. Norton & Company, 1995), p. 187.
5. Henry, p. 28.
6. David Herbert Donald, *Lincoln* (New York: Simon & Schuster, 1995), p. 284.
7. Donald, p. 420.
8. *The War of the Rebellion: A Compilation of the Official Records of the Union and Confederate Armies* (Carmel, IN: The Guild Press of Indiana, Inc., 1996) Series I, Vol. LI, Part I. CD-ROM version. Hereafter cited as OR.
9. OR, Series I, Vol. LI, Part I.
10. *The Papers of Jefferson Davis*, vol. 9, January–September, 1863, ed. Lynda Lasswell Crist (Baton Rouge: Louisiana State University Press, 1997) "President's message to the Senate and House of Representatives of the Confederate States," January 12, 1863.
11. "President's Message."
12. *The Collected Works of Abraham Lincoln*, vol. 6, ed. Roy P. Basler (New Brunswick, NJ: Abraham Lincoln Association, 1953–55), p. 357.
13. Donald, p. 48.
14. Thomas Ewing, Sr., to W.H. Seward, 13 January 1864. Library of Congress Manuscript Division, Washington, D.C. Thomas Ewing Family Papers O3171.
15. Edward S. Sanford to Edwin Stanton, 14 July 1863. OR, Series 1, Vol. XXVII, Part 2 (S#44).
16. John B. Jones, *A Rebel War Clerk's Diary at the Confederate States Capital* (Philadelphia: J.B. Lippincott & Co., 1866), p. 116.
17. James O. Hall, "The Dahlgren Papers: A Yankee Plot to Kill President Davis" in *Civil War Times Illustrated*, November 1983, p. 33.
18. Hall, p. 33.
19. Duane Schultz, *The Dahlgren Affair* (New York: W.W. Norton & Company, 1998), p. 175.
20. Schultz, p. 174.
21. William A. Tidwell, with James O. Hall and David Winfred Gaddy, *Come Retribution* (Jackson: University Press of Mississippi, 1998), p. 171.
22. Tidwell, with Hall and Gaddy, p. 172.
23. Steven Vincent Benet, *John Brown's Body* (New York: Rinehart & Company, 1954), p. 56.
24. Eli N. Evans, *Judah Benjamin: The Jewish Confederate* (New York: The Free Press, 1989), p. 162.

25. Eli N. Evans, *Judah Benjamin: The Jewish Confederate* (New York: The Free Press, 1989), p. 162.

26. William A. Tidwell, *April '65: Confederate Covert Action in the American Civil War* (Kent, OH: The Kent State University Press, 1995), p. 19.

27. *Canadian Historical Review* 2, 11 March 1921, p. 47.

28. OR, Series I, Vol. XVI, Part I, (S#93).

29. Williamson Simpson Oldham Memoir. Williamson Simpson Oldham Papers, Center for American History at the University of Texas at Austin, Boxes 2F164 and 2R130-2R131. Unpublished.

30. OR, Series I, Vol. XLI, Part I, (S#95).

31. Michael Fellman, *Citizen Sherman* (New York: Random House, 1995), p. 30.

Chapter Two

1. *The Life and Letters of Francis Lieber*, Thomas S. Perry, ed. (Boston: James R. Osgood, 1882), p. 134.

2. Papers of Francis Lieber, Henry E. Huntington Library, San Marino, California. Mss. L1 1–5222, boxes 21–53. Henry Halleck to Francis Lieber, 6 August 1862.

3. Lieber Papers, boxes 1–17 and 54–67.

4. Lieber Papers, boxes 1–17 and 54–67.

5. Lieber Papers, boxes 1–17 and 54–67.

6. *The Diary of George Templeton Strong*, Allan Nevins and Milton Halsey Thomas, eds. (New York: The Macmillan Company, 1952), vol. 3, p. 276.

7. Nevins and Thomas, p. 236.

8. Frank Freidel, *Francis Lieber, Nineteenth Century Liberal* (Baton Rouge: Louisiana State University Press, 1947), p. 122.

9. Freidel, p. 144

10. Perry, p. 161.

11. Nevins and Thomas, p. 236.

12. *New York Herald*, May 19 and 20, 1863.

13. *General Orders No. 100*, Adjutant General's Office, 1863 (Washington, D.C.: Government Printing Office, 1898). See also OR, Series I, Vol. 14 (S#120).

14. Letter from William T. Sherman to Ulysses S. Grant, 9 October 1864. OR, Series I, Vol. 39, Part 2.

15. Freidel, p. 336.

16. Mark Grimsley, *The Hard Hand of War: Union Military Policy Toward Southern Civilians, 1861–65* (Cambridge: Cambridge University Press, 1995), p. 181.

17. John Condon to Governor Frances W. Pickens. 11 January 1861. Leyburn Library, Washington and Lee University, Lexington, Virginia. The David Jamison Flavel Papers, O56.

18. Francis Lieber, "Instructions for the Government of the United States in the Field." Issued originally in 1863 as General Orders No. 100. (Washington, D.C.: United States Government Printing Office, 1898).

19. Jeffery K. Smart, "History of *Chemical and Biological Warfare: An American Perspective.*" In *Textbook of Military medicine: Medical Aspects of Chemical and Biological Warfare*. U.S. Army Soldier and Biological Chemical Command. (Washington D.C.: Office of the Surgeon General, 2000), p. 2.

20. William B. Thomas to Abraham Lincoln, 31 March 1863. The Abraham Lincoln Papers at the Library of Congress, series 1, reel 51.

21. *The Scientific American*, 28 March 1863, Vol. 8, Issue 13, p. 195.

22. *Official Records of the Union and Confederate Navies in the War of the Rebellion* (Washington, D.C.: Government Printing Office, 1912), p. 517.

23. *Official Records of the Union and Confederate Navies in the War of the Rebellion*, p. 518.

24. *Collected Poems of Herman Melville*, ed. Howard Vincent (Chicago: Packard, 1947), pp. 70–72.

25. OR, Series I, Vol. XXVIII, Part II, (S#47).

26. *The Trials for Treason at Indianapolis*, ed. Benn Pitman (Cincinnati: Moore, Wiltsach & Baldwin, 1865). Testimony of Richard Charles Bocking, pp. 190–191.

27. Pitman, *The Trials for Treason*, pp. 190–191.

28. Lieutenant General Ulysses S. Grant to Major General Edward Ord, 18 February 1865. OR, Series I, Vol. XLVI, Part II, (S# 86).

29. Milton F. Perry, *Infernal Machines: The Story of Confederate Submarine and Mine Warfare* (Baton Rouge: Louisiana State University Press, 1965), p. 20.

30. Brigadier General Gabriel J. Rains, Torpedo Book, Museum of the Confederacy, Eleanor Brockbrough Library, Manuscript Division, Richmond, Virginia. Unpublished.

31. Rains, Torpedo Book.

32. *U.S. Consular Dispatches* (Washington, D.C.: National Archives and Records Administration) roll T-491, p. 3.

33. New York Times, 18 May 1865. See also Edward Steers, Jr., "Risking the Wrath of God" in *North & South*, volume 3, number 7, September 2000, p. 81.

Chapter Three

1. James D. Horan, *Confederate Agent: A Discovery in History* (New York: Crown Publishing, Inc, 1954), p. 81.

2. Thomas Henry Hines pocket diary, August 8, 1865. Thomas Henry Hines Collection, University of Kentucky Special Collections and Archives, box 1a.

3. Horan, p. 97.

4. OR, Series II, Vol. VII (S#120).

5. George Fort Milton, *Abraham Lincoln and the Fifth Column* (New York: The Vanguard Press, 1942), p. 256.

6. OR, Series II, Vol. VII (S#120).

7. *The Continental Monthly*, January 1862, p. 573.

8. "Knights of the Golden Circle," in the *Columbia Encyclopedia*, sixth edition, (New York: Columbia University Press, 1950), p. 1063.

9. Felix G. Stidger, *Treason History of the Sons of Liberty* (Chicago: Felix Stidger, 1903), p. 157.

10. OR, Series II, Vol. VII (S#120).

11. Stidger, p. 84.

12. Horan, p. 97.

13. Stidger, p.10.

14. Stidger, p.15.

15. Stidger, p. 16.

16. Stidger, p. 17.

17. Stidger, p. 18.

18. Stidger, p. 20.

19. Stidger, p. 21.

20. Stidger, p. 21.

21. Stidger, p. 22.

22. Perryville, Kentucky, Battlefield Site: www.danvilleky.com/BoyleCounty/perryenh.htm.

23. OR, Series I, Vol. XVI, Part I (S#22).

24. Stidger, p. 22.

25. Stidger, p. 25.

26. Stidger, p. 25.

27. Stidger, p. 26.

28. Stidger, p. 26.

29. Stidger, p. 27.

30. Stidger, p. 28.

31. Stidger, p. 29.
32. Stidger, p. 30.
33. Stidger, p. 31.
34. Stidger, p. 32.
35. Stidger, p. 32.
36. OR, Series II, Vol. VII (S#120).
37. NARA RG (record group) 153, 16w3, nn2716, box 1608.
38. Stidger, pp. 34–35.
39. Stidger, p. 37.
40. Stidger, p. 40.
41. Stidger, p. 43.
42. NARA, RG 153, 16w3, nn2716, Box 1608.
43. NARA, RG 153, 16w3, nn2716, Box 1608.
44. Stidger, p. 67.
45. NARA, RG 153, 16w3, nn2716, Box 1608.
46. Horan, p. 99.
47. NARA, RG 153, 16w3, nn2716, Box 1608.
48. NARA, RG 153, 16w3, nn2716, Box 1608.
49. NARA, RG 153, 16w3, nn2716, Box 1608.
50. NARA, RG 153, 16w3, nn2716, Box 1608.
51. Stidger, p. 5.
52. NARA, RG 153, 16w3, nn2716, Box 1608.
53. NARA, RG 153, 16w3, nn2716, Box 1608.
54. NARA, RG 153, 16w3, nn2716, Box 1608.
55. NARA, RG 153, 16w3, nn2716, Box 1608.
56. NARA, RG 153, 16w3, nn2716, Box 1608.
57. NARA, RG 153, 16w3, nn2716, Box 1608.
58. NARA, RG 153, 16w3, nn2716, Box 1608.
59. NARA, RG 153, 16w3, nn2716, Box 1608.
60. Stidger, p. 82.
61. Stidger, p. 83.
62. NARA, RG 153, 16w3, nn2716, Box 1608.
63. NARA, RG 153, 16w3, nn2716, Box 1608.
64. NARA, RG 153, 16w3, nn2716, Box 1608.
65. NARA, RG 153, 16w3, nn2716, Box 1608.
66. Stidger, p. 104.
67. Stidger, p. 105.
68. Stidger, p. 107.
69. Stidger, p. 113.
70. Pitman, *The Trials for Treason at Indianapolis* (Cincinnati: Moore, Wiltsach & Baldwin, 1865), p. 17.
71. Stidger, p. 144.
72. Pitman, *The Trials for Treason at Indianapolis*, pp. 17–18.
73. Pitman, *The Trials for Treason at Indianapolis*, p. 18.
74. Stidger, p. 149.
75. Pitman, *The Trials for Treason at Indianapolis*, p. 27.
76. Pitman, *The Trials for Treason at Indianapolis*, p. 27.
77. Pitman, *The Trials for Treason at Indianapolis*, p. 27.
78. Pitman, *The Trials for Treason at Indianapolis*, p. 28.
79. Pitman, *The Trials for Treason at Indianapolis*, p. 28.
80. Milton, p. 313.
81. Stidger, p. 164.
82. William H. Rehnquist, "Remarks Delivered at the Indiana University School of Law," October 28, 1996. *Indiana Law Journal*, Vol. 72, 1997, p. 927.
83. Rehnquist.
84. Stidger, p. 178.

85. Rehnquist.
86. Rehnquist.

Chapter Four

1. *Diary of Charles Cooper, 1853*, The New York Public Library, Manuscripts and Archives Division, Astor, Lenox & Tilden Foundation.
2. Nat Brandt, *The Man Who Tried to Burn New York* (New York: toExcel, 1986), p. 80.
3. John W. Headley, *Confederate Operations in Canada and New York* (New York and Washington: The Neale Publishing Company, 1906), p. 264.
4. Headley, p. 266.
5. Headley, p. 266.
6. Headley, p. 267.
7. OR, Series I, Vol. XLIII, Part I (S#91).
8. Headley, p. 268.
9. Headley, p. 269.
10. Headley, p. 280.
11. Headley, p. 271.
12. Headley, p. 271.
13. Brandt, p. 101.
14. Headley, p. 272.
15. Headley, p. 272.
16. Headley, p. 272.
17. Headley, p. 272.
18. Brandt, p. 106.
19. Brandt, p. 116.
20. Headley, p. 275.
21. Headley, p. 275.
22. Headley, p. 275.
23. Headley, p. 276.
24. Brandt, p. 15.
25. Headley, pp. 275–276.
26. Headley, p. 276.
27. Headley, p. 276.
28. Headley, p. 277.
29. *New York Times*, 26 November 1864.
30. Brandt, p. 128.
31. Brandt, p. 131.
32. *New York Herald*, 29 November 1864.
33. NARA, RG 153, JAG, MM-3729.
34. *New York Times*, October 30, 1864.
35. Alfred E. Baker, *Fire Marshal's Report to the Mayor, 1 June–30 November, 1864*. (New York: Holman, 1865), pp. 4–5.
36. Headley, p. 277.
37. Headley, p. 277.
38. *New York Times*, 27 November 1864.
39. Headley, p. 278.
40. Headley, p. 278.
41. Headley, p. 280.
42. Headley, p. 280.
43. Report of Jacob Thompson, in *A Leaf From History* (Washington, D.C.: Union Republican Congressional Committee, December 3, 1864), Library of Congress, Rare Books Division.
44. Brandt, p. 144.
45. Brandt, p. 145.

46. Brandt, p. 145.
47. Brandt, p. 147.
48. Brandt, p. 148.
49. Headley, p. 323.
50. NARA, RG 153, JAG, MM-3729.
51. Brandt, p. 161–162; NARA, RG 153, JAG, MM-3729.
52. Brandt, p. 163–164; NARA, RG 153, JAG, MM-3729.
53. NARA, RG 153, JAG, MM-3729.
54. Brandt, p. 165.
55. Brandt, p. 165–166; NARA, RG 153, JAG, MM-3729.
56. Brandt, p. 170.
57. Brandt, p. 170.
58. Brandt, p. 194.
59. Lonnie R. Speer, *Portals to Hell: Military Prisons of the Civil War* (Mechanicsburg, PA: Stackpole Books, 1997), p. 35.
60. Brandt, p. 204.
61. Brandt, p. 205.
62. *Papers of Abraham Lincoln*, Vol. 192, 1865, March 11–22, Library of Congress.
63. Brandt, p. 213; NARA, RG 109, Union Provost Marshal's File, Lafayette Prison.
64. Brandt, p. 227.
65. NARA, RG 393, USACC (U.S. Army Continental Commands), Letters Received 1865.
66. Headley, p. 331
67. Headley, p. 402.
68. Headley, p. 405.
69. Headley, p. 405.
70. Headley, p. 409.
71. Headley, p. 428.
72. Headley, p. 429.
73. Headley, p. 429.
74. Headley, p. 430.
75. Headley, p. 439.
76. Headley, p. 468.
77. Headley, p. 440.
78. Headley, p. 472.
79. Headley, p. 449.
80. Headley, p. 450.
81. Headley, p. 460.

Chapter Five

1. *Bermuda Royal Gazette*, 25 April 1865.
2. *Bermuda Royal Gazette*, 25 April 1865.
3. *New York Times,* 30 May 1865.
4. *New York Times*, 30 May 1865.
5. *Bermuda Royal Gazette*, 25 April 1865.
6. Steers, p. 61.
7. Steers, p. 61.
8. H.H. Emmons to Attorney General James Speed, 22 April 1865. NARA, Records of the Office of Attorney General.
9. Pitman, *The Assassination of President Lincoln and the Trial of the Conspirators*, p. 56.
10. Pitman, *The Assassination of President Lincoln and the Trial of the Conspirators*, p. 55.
11. Pitman, *The Assassination of President Lincoln and the Trial of the Conspirators*, p. 54.
12. Pitman, *The Assassination of President Lincoln and the Trial of the Conspirators*, p. 55.
13. Pitman, *The Assassination of President Lincoln and the Trial of the Conspirators*, p. 55.

14. Pitman, *The Assassination of President Lincoln and the Trial of the Conspirators*, p. 55. To date, no record has been found of the trunks ever reaching Washington, D.C.

15. Steers, p. 64.

16. Steers, p. 61.

17. Steers, p. 60.

18. Nancy Disher Baird, *Luke Pryor Blackburn: Physician, Governor, Reformer* (Lexington: The University Press of Kentucky, 1979), p. vii.

19. Baird, p. 2.

20. Gerard T. Koppel, *Water for Gotham: A History* (Princeton, NJ: Princeton University Press, 2000), p. 321.

21. Koppel, p. 321.

22. Jefferson J. Polk, *Autobiography of Dr. J.J. Polk* (Louisville, KY, 1867), p. 33.

23. *Thesis of Luke Prior (sic) Blackburn, M.D.*, Transylvania University, pp. 4 and 15.

24. Centers for Disease Control, Division of Bacterial and Mycotic Diseases, Department of Health and Human Services, "Definition of Cholera."

25. *Louisville Courier Journal*, 17 September 1887.

26. "City of Natchez History," www.cityofnatchez.com.

27. Baird, p. 11.

28. Baird, p. 20.

29. Baird, p. 20.

30. Baird, p. 21.

31. Baird, p. 22.

32. Ben Perley Poore, *The Conspiracy Trial for the Murder of the President*, Four volumes (New York: Arno Press Reprint, 1972), pp. 409–419.

33. "American Consular Reports, Civil War Period" in *The Bermuda Historical Quarterly*, No. 19, Spring 1862, p. 25.

34. Steers, "Risking the Wrath of God," p. 65.

35. Douglas Southall Freeman, *Lee's Dispatches: Unpublished Letters of Robert E. Lee to Jefferson Davis* (Baton Rouge: Louisiana State University Press, 1994), pp. 302–304.

36. Freeman, p. 302–304.

37. Freeman, p. 302–304.

38. Steers, p. 67.

39. Kensey Johns Stewart to Jefferson Davis, 12 December 1864. NARA RG 109.

40. Steers, p. 71.

41. Conrad, p. 72.

42. William A. Tidwell, with James O. Hall and David W. Gaddy, *Come Retribution: The Confederate Secret Service and the Assassination of Abraham Lincoln*, p. 291.

43. Thomas Nelson Conrad, *A Confederate Spy* (New York: J. S. Olgilvie, 1892), p. 56.

44. Judah P. Benjamin to Jacob Thompson, 30 December 1864. Eleanor Brockenbrough Library, Museum of the Confederacy, Richmond, Virginia.

45. Tidwell, Hall and Gaddy, p. 203.

46. Diary of Edwin Gray Lee in Canada, William A. Perkins Library, Duke University. Rare Book, Manuscript and Special Collections Library, box 90185.

47. Diary of Edwin Gray Lee in Canada.

48. *Letter Books of Confederate State Papers, Canada: February 15, 1864–January 8, 1865.* Library of Congress.

49. Alexandra Lee Levin, *This Awful Drama: General Edwin Gray Lee, C.S.A., and His Family* (New York: Vantage Press, 1987), pp. 134–135.

50. Levin, p. 140.

51. Diary of Edwin Gray Lee in Canada.

52. Levin, p. 144.

53. Headley, p. 256.

54. Headley, p. 259.

55. "Canadian Confederation, Influence of the American Civil War," National Library of Canada.

56. Levin, p. 147.

57. Levin, p. 148.

58. Diary of Edwin Gray Lee in Canada.

59. Susan Lee Blackford, *Letters from Lee's Army: Or Memoirs of Life in and Out of the Army of Virginia During the War Between the States* (Lincoln: University of Nebraska Press, 1998), p. 243.

60. Steers, p. 65.

61. Steers, p. 65.

62. Benn Pitman, *The Assassination of President Lincoln and the Trial of the Conspirators,* "Introduction of Pestilence," May 29, 1865, p. 55.

63. *Bermuda Royal Gazette*, 25 April 1865.

64. *Bermuda Royal Gazette*, 25 April 1865.

65. *Bermuda Royal Gazette*, 25 April 1865.

66. *Bermuda Royal Gazette*, 25 April 1865.

67. *New York Times*, 26 May 1865.

68. Steers, p. 61.

69. *New York Times*, 26 May 1865.

70. Steers, p. 61.

71. Steers, p. 68.

72. A verse from a parody of the Civil War song "John Brown's Body," which was sung to the tune of "The Battle Hymn of the Republic." Allegedly, after the capture of Jefferson Davis, Union soldiers taunted him with the verse.

73. NARA, *Book With Index to Secret Service Payments, War Department, 1861–70, Levi C. Turner-Lafayette C. Baker Papers, Records of the Adjutant General's Office.*

74. Steers, p. 68.

75. *New York Times*, 30 May 1865.

76. Luke P. Blackburn to Andrew Johnson, 4 September 1867. Andrew Johnson Presidential Papers, Manuscript Division, Microfilm Series 1, reel 28, NARA.

Chapter Six

1. *New York Times*, 5 August 1872.

2. OR, Series I, Vol. LXI, Part I (S#95).

3. Original in possession of Mr. and Mrs. Richard S. McCulloch (unpublished). The family inserted the letter "c" to the name "McCulloh" at the turn of the century, reverting to the original spelling of the name. See also Milton Halsey Thomas, "Professor McCulloh of Princeton, Columbia and Points South" in *Princeton University Library Chronicle* (Princeton, New Jersey, 1947), Vol. 9, p. 23.

4. Robert McCaughey, Columbia University Archivist.

5. *The Diary of George Templeton Strong*, Allan Nevins & Milton Halsey Thomas, eds. (New York: The Macmillan Company, 1952) vol. 3, pp. 362–363.

6. "Columbia of Yesterday" in *The Columbian* (Princeton, N.J., 1926) Princeton University Archives.

7. "Confederate Ordnance During the Civil War" in the *Journal of U.S. Artillery*, CV 12, p. 20.

8. Ralph W. Donnelly, "Scientists of the Confederate Nitre and Mining Bureau" in *Civil War History,* 1A, Volume 2, Number 4 (Iowa City, IA, 1956); Virginia Historical Society, General Collection E461 C5, p. 19.

9. Donnelley, p. 19.

10. "Testimonial of Charles B. Fisk" in Milton Halsey Thomas, "Professor McCulloh of Princeton, Columbia and Points South" in *Princeton University Library Chronicle* (Princeton, New Jersey, 1947), p. 19.

11. Thomas, p. 19.

12. Thomas, p. 19.

13. Richard McCulloh to Isabella McCulloh, 24 November 1841. McCulloh family archives.

14. Thomas, p. 20
15. Thomas, p. 20.
16. Nevins and Thomas, Strong diary, *The Turbulent Fifties*, p. 200.
17. Nevins and Thomas, Strong diary, p. 235.
18. Thomas, p. 22.
19. John McCulloch to Margaretta Grace Brown McCulloch, date illegible, possibly 19 March 1895. McCulloch family archives (unpublished).
20. John McCulloch letter (unpublished).
21. John McCulloch letter (unpublished).
22. Oldfields School archivist Meg Gallucci to Jane Singer, January 30, 2001.
23. McCulloch family archives.
24. Nevins and Thomas, Strong diary, *The Civil War*, p. 570.
25. Nevins and Thomas, Strong diary, *The Civil War*, p. 570.
26. Nevins and Thomas, Strong diary, *The Civil War*, p. 573.
27. John Torrey to Asa Gray, 15 July 1863. Columbia University Archives.
28. Emory M. Thomas, *Robert E. Lee* (New York: W.W. Norton & Company, 1995), pp. 307–308.
29. Sally Brock Putnam, *Richmond During the War* (Lincoln: University of Nebraska Press, 1996), p. 250.
30. Letters received, Confederate War Department, M346, Roll 623, NARA.
31. Letters received, Confederate War Department, M346, Roll 623, NARA.
32. Letters received, Confederate War Department, M346, Roll 623, NARA.
33. Letters received, Confederate War Department, M346, Roll 623, NARA.
34. OR, Series IV, Vol. III (S#129).
35. William A. Tidwell, *April '65 : Confederate Covert Action in the American Civil War* (Kent, OH: The Kent State University Press, 1995), p. 35.
36. Dr. Linda McCurdy, Director of Research Services in the Rare Book, Manuscript and Special Collections Library at Duke University to Jane Singer, May 9, 2001.
37. A. J. Hanna, *Flight Into Oblivion* (Richmond: Johnson Publishing Company, 1938), p. 127.
38. Benn Pitman, *The Assassination of President Lincoln and the Trial of the Conspirators* (Cincinnati: Moore, Wiltsach and Baldwin, 1865) "Introduction of Pestilence," May 29, 1865, pp. 47–49.
39. Pitman, *The Assassination of President Lincoln and the Trial of the Conspirators*, p. 47–49.
40. Nevins and Thomas, Strong diary, *The Civil War*, p. 597.
41. OR, Series IV, Vol. III (S#129).
42. *New York Herald*, 29 May 1865.
43. *New York Tribune*, 29 May 1865.
44. *New York Herald*, 29 May 1865.
45. Nevins and Thomas, Strong diary, *The Civil War*, p. 601.
46. "Telegrams Collected by the Secretary of War," M-473, Reel 118, Frame 724, NARA.
47. Brevet Lt. Colonel Richard A. Watts, "The Trial of the Lincoln Conspirators" in *In Pursuit of…Continuing Research in the Field of the Lincoln Assassins: Compiled from the newsletters of the Surratt Society* (Clinton, MD: The Surratt Society, 1990), pp. 208–209.
48. Nevins and Thomas, Strong diary, *The Post-War Years*, p. 20.
49. *Department of Collections Record*, RG 42, Library of Virginia, Richmond, Virginia.
50. *Harper's Weekly*, 18 November 1865. Also in the McCulloch family archives.
51. Scrapbook of Richard Sears McCulloh, McCulloch family archives (unpublished).
52. Robert E. Lee to Richard S. McCulloh, 23 May 1866 (unpublished). Leyburn Library of Washington and Lee University, Lexington, Virginia.
53. Richard S. McCulloh to Robert E. Lee, 28 May 1868 (unpublished). Leyburn Library of Washington and Lee University, Lexington, Virginia.
54. Hudson Strode, *Jefferson Davis, Tragic Hero: 1864–1899, The Last Twenty-Five Years* (New York: Harcourt, Brace & Company, 1964), p. 354. The letter cited is not sourced. This author has attempted to find the letter. To date it has not been located.
55. Strode, p. 354.

56. Scrapbook of Richard Sears McCulloh, McCulloch family archives (unpublished).

57. Richard McCulloh to John McCulloch, 29 November 1885. McCulloch family archives (unpublished).

Chapter Seven

1. Thomas C. DeLeon, *Four Years in Rebel Capitals* (The Gossip Printing Company, 1892). See A. A. Hoehling and Mary Hoehling, *The Day Richmond Died* (Lanham, MD: Madison Books, 1981), p. 104.

2. Constance Carey, *Recollections Grave and Gay* (New York: Charles Scribner's Sons, 1911). See Hoehling, p. 104.

3. Robert E. Lee telegram to Jefferson Davis, 2 April 1865. Robert Edward Lee Papers, Virginia State Library, Richmond, Virginia.

4. John B. Jones, *A Rebel War Clerk's Diary at the Confederate Capital*, vol. II (Philadelphia: J.B. Lippincott & Company, 1866), p. 465.

5. Sally Brock Putnam, *Richmond During the War* (Lincoln: University of Nebraska Press, 1996), p. 368.

6. Hoehling, p. 143.

7. Putnam, p. 364.

8. Putnam, p. 365.

9. Jones, p. 468.

10. Brigadier General Edward H. Ripley, *Final Scenes at the Capture and Occupation of Richmond* (New York: Military Order of the Loyal Legion of the United States [MOLLUS], Volume III, December 5, 1906), pp. 472–502.

11. Major Godfrey Weitzel, *Richmond Occupied: Entry of the United States Forces Into Richmond, Virginia, April 3, 1865* (Richmond: Richmond Civil War Centennial Committee, 1865).

12. Putnam, p. 368.

13. See Hoehling, p. 155.

14. Putnam, p. 364.

15. Putnam, p. 369.

16. Putnam, p. 372.

17. Otto Eisenschiml, ed., *Vermont General: The Unusual Experiences of Edward Hastings Ripley* (New York: The Devin-Adair Company, 1960), p. 306. See also Ripley, p. 472–502.

18. Otto Eisenschiml, ed., *Vermont General: The Unusual War Experiences of Edward Hastings Ripley* (New York: The Devin-Adair Company, 1960), pp. 472–502.

19. Tidwell, *April '65 : Confederate Covert Action in the American Civil War*, p. 161.

20. *Union Provost Marshal's Civilian Files*, RG 109, NARA.

21. Snyder, William A. *Union Provost Marshal's Citizen File*, RG 109, NARA.

22. Tidwell, p. 161.

23. Eisenschiml, p. 306.

24. Eisenschiml, p. 307.

25. Eisenschiml, p. 308.

26. Ripley, p. 499.

27. Eisenschiml, p. 308.

28. Tidwell, p. 240, note 21.

29. "Statement of George A. Atzerodt to Provost Marshal James McPhail," 1 May 1865 in *The Surratt Courier*.

30. Tidwell with Hall and Gaddy, *Come Retribution*, p. 418.

31. "Statement of George A. Atzerodt to Provost Marshal James McPhail."

32. Percy C. Powell, *Lincoln Day By Day: A Chronology, 1809–1865* (Dayton, OH: Morningside Press, 1991) Entry for April 10, 1865.

33. Jay Winik, *April 1865, The Month That Saved America* (New York: Harper Collins, 2001), p. 158.

34. Kristen Stephenson, Ozarks History Syllabus.

35. Deborah and George Rule, "Missouri Time Line," www.civilwarstlouis.com.

36. Thomas L. Snead, "The First Year of the War in Missouri" in *Battles and Leaders of the Civil War* (New York: Century Publishing, 1887–1888), p. 234.

37. Randolph Harrison Dyer to his sister, 12 August 1861. Western Historical Manuscript Collection, C3193, University of Missouri at Columbia.

38. "The Battle of Oak Hills, Missouri, or Wilson's Creek," Missouri Division of the Sons of Confederate Veterans Battle Histories, July 1998.

39. John J. Gueguen, Jr., 'The Battle of Lexington, Missouri," www.historiclexington.com/battle.html.

40. R.S. Bevier, *History of the First and Second Missouri Confederate Brigades* (St. Louis: Bryan, Brand & Company, 1879), pp. 56–57.

41. "The Ballad of Elkhorn Tavern," collected from Ethel Doxey of Carroll County, Arkansas. In *Ballads and Songs*: Collected by the Missouri *Folklore Society*, ed. H.M. Belden.

42. Petersburg National Battlefield Information Service.

43. Lonnie R. Speer, *Portals to Hell: Military Prisons of the Civil War* (Mechanicsburg, PA: Stackpole Books, 1997), p. 47.

44. civilwarstlouis.com.

45. *Unfiled Papers and Slips Belonging in Confederate Compiled Service Records*, M-347, Reel 169 (9 in alphabetical order) NARA.

46. *Unfiled Papers and Slips Belonging in Confederate Compiled Service Records*, M-347, Reel 169 (9 in alphabetical order) NARA.

47. Daniel Moran, "Prisoner Exchange" in Aldie's *Civil War Daily* (October 15, 2002.)

48. RG 109, Entries 236–239, *Court Martial Archives, Gratiot Prison*, NARA.

49. Thomas Harney to Captain James A. Dwight, 18 April 1863. *Unfiled Papers and Slips Belonging in Confederate Compiled Service Records*, M-347, Reel 169 (9 in alphabetical order) NARA.

50. *Unfiled Papers and Slips Belonging in Confederate Compiled Service Records*, M-347, Reel 169 (9 in alphabetical order) NARA.

51. *Unfiled Papers and Slips Belonging in Confederate Compiled Service Records*, M-347, Reel 169 (9 in alphabetical order) NARA.

52. Tidwell, with Hall and Gaddy, p. 157.

53. Tidwell, with Hall and Gaddy, p. 157.

54. Brigadier General Gabriel J. Rains, "Torpedo Book," Eleanor Brockenbrough Library, Museum of the Confederacy, Richmond, Virginia (unpublished).

55. Tidwell, Hall and Gaddy, p. 158.

56. Milton F. Perry, *Infernal Machines*, p. 121.

57. Tidwell, Hall and Gaddy, p. 419.

58. Tidwell, *April '65*, p. 164.

59. Thomas J. Evans and James M. Moyer, *Mosby's Confederacy: A Guide to the Roads and Sites of Colonel John Singleton Mosby* (Shippensburg, PA: White Mane Publishing Company, Inc., 1991), pp. 49–50.

60. James J. Williamson, *Mosby's Rangers: A Record of the Operations of the Forty-Third Battalion Virginia Cavalry* (New York: Ralph B. Kenyon, 1896), p. 263.

61. Williamson, p. 367.

62. OR, Series I, Vol. LXI, Part I (S#95).

63. OR, Series I, Vol. LXI, Part I (S#95).

64. OR, Series I, Vol. LXI, Part I (S#95).

65. OR, Series I, Vol. LXI, Part I (S#95).

66. RG 393, Part 4, Entry 1465, NARA.

67. RG 393, Part 4, Entry 1465, NARA.

68. RG 393, Part 4, Entry 1465, NARA.

69. Joan L. Chaconas, "The Old Capital Prison," in the Surratt Society News (Clinton, MD., Surratt Society, April 1997).

70. RG 393, Part 4, Entry 1457, NARA.

71. Lonnie R. Speer, *Portals to Hell: Military Prisons in the Civil War* (Mechanicsburg, PA: Stackpole Books, 1997), p. 246.

72. Michael Horigan, *Elmira, Death Camp of the North* (Mechanicsburg, PA: Stackpole Books, 2002), p. 101.

73. Speer, p. 246.

Chapter Eight

1. Nancy Disher Baird, *Luke Pryor Blackburn: Physician, Governor, Reformer* (Lexington: The University Press of Kentucky, 1979), p.41.

2. Robert E. Lee, Jr., *Recollections and Letters of Robert E. Lee* (New York: Doubleday, Page & Company, 1904), p. 431.

3. *Louisville Courier Journal,* 10 April 1895. Thomas A. Harris obituary.

4. NARA, RG 94, *Office of the Adjutant General. Index of Secret Service Payments, 1861–1870.*

5. Felix Stidger to Francis Van Pelt, 23 December 1903 (unpublished).

6. Stidger to Van Pelt.

7. Stidger to Van Pelt.

8. *Chicago Sun Times,* May 15, 1908.

9. Andrew Herrmann, *Chicago Sun Times,* June 2, 2002.

Appendix A: Coda

1. Otto Eisenschiml, *Vermont General: The Unusual War Experiences of Edward Hastings Ripley, 1862–1865* (New York: The Devin-Adair Co., 1960), p. 308.

2. Eisenschiml, p. 308.

3. Eisenschiml, p. 295.

4. Eisenschiml, p. 311.

Appendix B: Arc of a Bomber: The Life and Death of William Stephen Deupree

1. Deupree family chronicles (unpublished) furnished by Susan Deupree Jones.

2. Deupree family chronicles.

3. "Confederate Soldiers who Served in Organizations from the State of Virginia" NARA RG M324-15, microfilm E 581.4, N37.

4. OR, Series I, Vol. XLII, Part I (S#87).

5. OR, Series I, Vol. XLVI, Part III (S#97).

6. Deupree family chronicles.

7. Deupree family chronicles.

8. OR, Series I, Vol. XLII, Part III (S#89).

9. Deupree family chronicles.

10. Deupree family chronicles.

Bibliography

Books

Baird, Nancy Disher. *Luke Pryor Blackburn: Physician, Governor, Reformer.* Lexington: The University Press of Kentucky, 1979.

Basler, Roy P., ed. *The Collected Works of Abraham Lincoln.* New Brunswick, NJ: Abraham Lincoln Association, 1953–55.

Benet, Stephen Vincent. *John Brown's Body.* New York: Rinehart, 1954.

Bevier, R.S. *History of the First and Second Missouri Confederate Brigades.* St. Louis: Bryan, Brand & Company, 1879.

Blackford, Susan Lee. *Letters from Lee's Army: Or Memoirs of Life in and Out of the Army of Virginia During the War Between the States.* Lincoln: University of Nebraska Press, 1998.

Brandt, Nat. *The Man Who Tried to Burn New York.* New York: toExcel, 1986.

Carey, Constance. *Recollections Grave and Gay.* New York: Charles Scribner's Sons, 1911.

Conrad, Thomas Nelson. *A Confederate Spy.* New York: J. S. Olgilvie, 1892.

Crawford, J. Marshall. *Mosby and His Men.* Geo. W. Carleton, & Co., 1867.

Crist, Lynda Lasswell, ed. *The Papers of Jefferson Davis.* II volumes. Baton Rouge: Louisiana State University Press, 1997.

DeLeon, Thomas C. *Four Years in Rebel Capitals.* The Gossip Printing Company, 1892.

Donald, David Herbert. *Lincoln.* New York: Simon & Schuster, 1995.

Eisenschiml, Otto, ed. *Vermont General: The Unusual War Experiences of Edward Hastings Ripley.* New York: The Devin-Adair, 1960.

Evans, Eli N. *Judah Benjamin.* New York: Free Press, 1989.

Evans, Thomas J., and James M. Moyer. *Mosby's Confederacy. A Guide to the Roads and Sites of Colonel John Singleton Mosby.* Shippensburg, PA: White Mane, 1991.

Fellman, Michael. *Citizen Sherman.* New York: Random House, 1996.

Freeman, Douglas Southall, ed. *Lee's Dispatches: Unpublished Letters of Robert E. Lee to Jefferson Davis.* Baton Rouge: Louisiana State University Press, 1994.

Friedel, Frank. *Francis Lieber, Nineteenth Century Liberal.* Baton Rouge: Louisiana State University Press, 1947.

Gray, Wood. *The Hidden Civil War, The Story of the Copperheads.* New York: Viking Press, 1942.

Grimsley, Mark. *The Hard Hand of War: Union Military Policy Toward Southern Civilians, 1861–1865.* Cambridge, MA: Cambridge University Press, 1995.

Hanna, A.J. *Flight Into Oblivion.* Richmond: Johnson Publishing Company, 1938.

Headley, John W. *Confederate Operations in Canada and New York.* New York: Neale, 1906.

Henry, Ralph Selph. *The Story of the Confederacy.* New York: Konecky & Konecky, 1931.

Hoehling A.A., and Mary Hoehling. *The Day Richmond Died.* Boulder, CO: Madison Books, 1981.

Horan, James D. *Confederate Agent, a Discovery in History.* New York: Crown, 1954.

Horigan, Michael. *Elmira, Death Camp of the North.* Mechanicsburg, PA: Stackpole Books, 2002.

Jones, John B. *A Rebel War Clerk's Diary.* 2 volumes. Philadelphia: J.B. Lippincott, 1866.

Koppel, Gerard T. *Water for Gotham: A History.* Princeton, NJ: Princeton University Press, 2000.

Lee, Robert E., Jr. *Recollections and Letters of Robert E. Lee.* New York: Doubleday, Page, 1904.

Levin, Alexandra Lee. *This Awful Drama: General Edwin Gray Lee, C.S.A., and His Family.* New York: Vantage Press, 1987

Lincoln, Abraham. *Collected Work.* Volume 6. New Brunswick, NJ: Abraham Lincoln Association, 1953–55.

Milton, George Fort. *Abraham Lincoln and the Fifth Column.* New York: The Vanguard Press, 1942.

Nevins, Allan and Milton Halsey Thomas, eds. *The Diary of George Templeton Strong.* Four volumes. New York: Macmillan, 1952.

Ownsbey, Betty J. *Alias "Paine."* Jefferson, NC: McFarland, 1993.

Parker, Sandra, V. *Richmond's Civil War Prisons.* Lynchburg, VA: H.E. Howard, 1990.

Perry, Milton F. *Infernal Machines: The Story of Confederate Submarine and Mine Warfare.* Baton Rouge: Louisiana State University Press, 1965.

Perry, Thomas S. *The Life and Letters of Francis Lieber.* Boston: James R. Osgood, 1882.

Pitman, Benn, ed. *The Trials for Treason at Indianapolis.* Cincinnati: Moore, Wilstach and Baldwin, 1865.

Pitman, Benn, ed. *The Assassination of President Lincoln and the Trial of the Conspirators.* Cincinnati: Moore, Wilstach & Baldwin, 1865.

Polk, Jefferson J. *Autobiography of Dr. J. J. Polk.* Louisville, KY, 1867.

Poore, Ben Perley. *The Conspiracy Trial for the Murder of the President.* New York: Arno Press, 1972.

Powell, Percy C. *Lincoln Day By Day: A Chronology, 1809–1865.* Dayton: Morningside Press, 1991.

Putnam, Sally Brock. *Richmond During the War.* Lincoln: University of Nebraska Press, 1996.

Ripley, Brigadier General Edward H. *The Capture and Occupation of Richmond, April 3, 1865.* New York: G.P. Putnam & Sons, 1907.

Rukeyser, Muriel. *The Soul and Body of John Brown.* The Columbia Book of Civil War Poetry. New York: Columbia University Press, 1994.

Schultz, Duane. *The Dahlgren Affair.* New York: W.W. Norton, 1998.

Speer, Lonnie R. *Portals to Hell, Military Prisons of the Civil War.* Mechanicsburg, PA: Stackpole Books, 1997.

Stidger, Felix Grundy. *Treason History of the Order of the Sons of Liberty.* Chicago: Felix Stidger, 1903.

Strode, Hudson. *Jefferson Davis, Tragic Hero: 1864–1899, The Last Twenty-Five Years.* New York: Harcourt Brace & Company, 1964.

Thomas, Emory M. *Robert E. Lee.* New York: W.W. Norton, 1995.

Tidwell, William A., with James O. Hall and David Winfred Gaddy. *Come Retribution.* Jackson: University Press of Mississippi, 1988.

Tidwell, William A. *April '65: Confederate Covert Action in the American Civil War.* Kent, OH: Kent State University Press, 1995.

Vincent, Howard, ed. *Collected Poems of Herman Melville.* Chicago: Packard, 1947.

Williamson, James J. *Mosby's Rangers: A Record of the Operations of the Forty-Third Battalion Virginia Cavalry.* New York: Ralph B. Kenyon, 1896.

Winik, Jay. *April 1865: The Month That Saved America.* New York: Harper Collins, 2001.

Manuscripts and Articles

"American Consular Reports-Civil War Period." *Bermuda Historical Quarterly* 19, Spring 1962.

Baker, Alfred E. *Fire Marshal's Report to the Mayor, June 1–November 30, 1864*. New York: Holman, 1865.

Chaconas, Joan C. "The Old Capital Prison." *Surratt Society News*, April 1997.

"Columbia of Yesterday," *Columbian 1926*. Columbia University Archives.

"Confederate ordnance During the Civil War." *Journal of U.S. Artillery*. CV 12.

Davis, Jefferson. Papers. January–September, 1863. Rice University, ms–43.

Donnelly, Ralph W. "Scientists of the Confederate Nitre and Mining Bureau." Virginia Historical Society.

Dyer, Randolph Harrison. Letters. Western Historical Manuscript Collection, University of Missouri, Columbia C3193.

Flave, David Jamison. Papers. Leyburn Library, Washington & Lee University, Lexington Virginia.

Hall, James O. "The Dahlgren Papers: A Yankee Plot to Kill President Davis." *Civil War Times Illustrated*, November 1983.

Hines, Thomas Henry. Collection. University of Kentucky Special Collections and Archives, 46m 97. Box 1a contains Pocket Diary (1865), entry for August 5, 1865.

Johnson, Andrew. Presidential Papers. NARA Manuscript Division, microfilm series I, reel 28.

Latrobe, Benjamin Henry. Elevations and Drawings for the Virginia "Penitentiary House." Library of Virginia, Department of Corrections Collection, Record Group 42.

Lee, Edwin Gray. "Diary of Edwin Gray Lee in Canada." William R. Perkins Library, Duke University, Rare Book, Manuscript and Special Collections Library. Box 90185, call number 3148.

Lee, Robert Edward, Papers. Virginia State Library, Richmond, Virginia.

Leland, Charles G. "The Knights of the Golden Circle." *The Continental Monthly: Devoted to Literature and National Policy*, Vol. 1, Issue 1, January 1862. New York and Boston: J.R. Gilmore. Page 573.

Lieber, Francis. Papers, 1815–1888. Henry E. Huntington Library, Call no. mss LI 1–5222, boxes 21–53.

Oldham, Williamson Simpson. Papers. Center for American History, University of Texas, boxes 2F164 and 2R130–2R131.

Report of Jacob Thompson in *A Leaf from History*. Washington D.C.: Union Republican Congressional Committee, December 3, 1864. Library of Congress, Rare Books Division.

Rains, Brigadier General Gabriel J. "Torpedo Book." Museum of the Confederacy, Eleanor Brockenbrough Library, Manuscript Division.

"Richmond Occupied: Entry of the United States Forces into Richmond, Virginia, April 3, 1865." Richmond Civil War Centennial Committee, 1965.

Smart, Jeffrey K. *History of Chemical and Biological Warfare: An American Perspective*. Washington, D.C.: Office of the Surgeon General & Department of the Army, 1997.

"Statement of George A. Atzerodt to Provost Marshall James McPhail." Surratt Society, Clinton, Maryland. Discovered by Joan L. Chaconas in the papers of William O. Doster, now in private hands.

Steers, Jr., Edward. "Risking the Wrath of God." *North and South*, September 2000, Volume 3, Number 7.

Surrat Society. "In Pursuit of…Continuing Research in the Field of the Lincoln Assassins." Compiled from the newsletters of the Surratt Society, Clinton, Maryland, 1990.

Newspapers

Bermuda Royal Gazette, April 25, 1865.
Harper's Weekly, November 18, 1865.
Louisville Courier Journal, September 17, 1887.
Louisville Courier Journal, April 19, 1895.
New York Herald, May 19, 1863.
New York Herald, May 20, 1863.
New York Herald, November 29, 1864.
New York Times, November 26, 1864.
New York Times, November 27, 1864.
New York Times, November 30, 1864.
New York Times, May 18, 1865.
New York Times, May 26, 1865.
New York Times, May 30, 1865.
New York Times, August 6, 1872.

National Archives

O.R. or Official Rebellion Records
    Series I, Volume LI, Part 1.
    Series I, Volume XLVl, Part 1 (S#95).
    Series I, Volume XLVl, Part 2 (S#86).
    Series II, Volume VII (S#120).
    Series I, Volume XVI, Part 1 (S#22).
    Series I, Volume XLIII, Part 1 (S#91).
    Series IV, Volume III (S#129).
    Series I, Volume IV, Part 3.
Confederate Compiled Service Records, M437, roll 169.
General Records of the Department of Justice, 1790–1989, RG 60.
General Records of the Department of Justice, 1790–1989, Records of the Office of the Attorney General, RG 60.3.
Office of the Adjutant General, Index of Secret Service Payments, 1861–1870, RG 94.
Records of the Immediate Office of the Judge Advocate General, 1808–1891. RG 153 JAG, mm-3729.
Records of the Office of the Assistant Judge Advocate General. Record Group 153 16w3, mm2716, box 1808.
Records of the United States Army Continental Commands. RG 393, Part IV, Entry 1465 and RG 393.12, Part IV, Entry 1457, Volume II.
Records of the United States Army Continental Commands, Records of Provost Marshal Field Organization, 1861–1870. RG 393.12
Telegrams Collected by the Secretary of War, Volumes 246–247, m-473, reel 118, frame 724.
Unfiled papers and Slips Belonging in the Confederate Compiled Service Records, M-347, reel 169.
Union Provost Marshal's Citizen File, RG 109.
Union Provost Marshal's Civilian Files, RG 109.

Index